Turkey's Road to European Union Membership

Enlargement to Turkey is arguably the greatest challenge facing the European Union today. After the narrowly averted "train crash" over Cyprus in 2006, the second election victory of the Justice and Development Party in July 2007 opened new prospects for Turkish-EU relations. But in an EU emphasising a collective identity based on shared civilisational values, Turkey's European credentials have been increasingly called into question. Amending national identity through political change has become the key to the success or failure of the Turkish integration project. This volume examines the EU role in strengthening the domestic pro-reform coalition within Turkey, the paradox—and potential limits—of Turkey's europeanising Islamists, and the impact of Europeanisation through conditionality, including a case study of Turkish policy towards the Cyprus Question. Also addressed are the Western stereotypes of Turkish identity influencing the country's EU prospects, notably concerning the role of Islam in precipitating acts of political violence and its association with sexual and political violence in the discourse of European opponents of Turkish accession. In addition, the dynamics of EU accession negotiations are analysed and the potential role of a norm-driven rhetorical strategy in promoting Turkish accession as a moral and democratic imperative is discussed.

This book was previously published as a special issue of the *Journal of Southern Europe and the Balkans*.

Susannah Verney is Lecturer in International and European Studies, University of Athens and Editor, *South European Society & Politics*.

Kostas Ifantis is Associate Professor of International Relations, University of Athens.

Turkey's Road to European Union Membership

National Identity and Political Change

Edited by
Susannah Verney and Kostas Ifantis

Routledge
Taylor & Francis Group

LONDON AND NEW YORK

First published 2009 by Routledge
2 Park Square, Milton Park, Abingdon, Oxon, OX14 4RN

Simultaneously published in the USA and Canada by Routledge
270 Madison Avenue, New York, NY 10016

Routledge is an imprint of the Taylor & Francis Group, an informa business

Transferred to Digital Printing 2009

Typeset in Palatino 10/12pt by Alden Prepress Services, Northhampton

British Library Cataloguing in Publication Data
A catalogue record for this book is available from the British Library

ISBN 10: 0-415-46619-9 (hbk)
ISBN 10: 0-415-57469-2 (pbk)

ISBN 13: 978-0-415-46619-6 (hbk)
ISBN 13: 978-0-415-57469-3 (pbk)

CONTENTS

Contributors

SINEM ACIKMESE is a Research Assistant at Ankara University.

MUSTAFA AYDIN is a Professor and Chair of the Department of International Relations at the University of Economics and Technology, Ankara.

KOSTAS IFANTIS is Associate Professor of International Relations, University of Athens.

LUIGI NARBONE is an official of the European Commission.

ZIYA ÖNIŞ is Professor of European Politics and International Relations at Koç University, Istanbul.

ERSIN KALAYCIOĞLU is a Political Scientist at Sabanci University, Istanbul.

NATHALIE TOCCI is a Senior Fellow at the Istituto Affari Internazionali, Rome.

KIVANÇ ULUSOY is an Assistant Professor at the Faculty of Political Sciences of Istanbul University, Istanbul.

SUSANNAH VERNEY is Lecturer in International & European Studies at the University of Athens and Editor of *South European Society & Politics*.

HAKAN YILMAZ is Professor of Political Science, Bogazici University, Istanbul.

National identity and political change on Turkey's road to EU membership

SUSANNAH VERNEY

Reluctant partners

Turkey's long march to European Union began almost 50 years ago. In July 1959, Turkey became only the second non-founder member of the then EEC to ask to participate in the European integration process, submitting its application for an Association just weeks after Greece. The Ankara Agreement, signed in 1963, inaugurated economic integration between Turkey and the EEC while leaving Turkey outside the political decision-making process. From the start, the Turkish relationship with the EEC was framed in a prospect of eventual full membership. Thus, according to Article 28 of the Association,

> As soon as the operation of the Agreement has advanced far enough to justify envisaging full acceptance by Turkey of the obligations arising out of the Treaty establishing the Community, the Contracting Parties shall examine the possibility of the accession of Turkey to the Community.

This was reinforced by the preamble to the Agreement, which stated that

> the support given by the European Economic Community to the efforts of the Turkish people to improve their standard of living will facilitate the accession of Turkey to the Community at a later date.

Despite this apparent statement of intent, another 41 years were to pass before Turkey opened negotiations for accession to what was by then the European Union. In the meantime, five successive Enlargements had resulted in 19 other states gaining full membership ahead of Turkey (followed by another two states in 2007). This long delay can be attributed to reluctance on both sides.

In the 1970s, it was Turkey which was the hesitant partner. The Association Agreement had become the object of growing domestic criticism, as industrialists feared a move away from a national economic development strategy based on import substitution. A particular cause of contention was the limits on Turkish textile imports unilaterally imposed by the EC in 1978. Meanwhile, there had been unrealistic expectations of EC aid, with the Turkish government requesting $8 billion, when the EC was prepared to offer $600 million.[1] Disappointment with

---

[1] A. Eralp, 'Turkey and the EC in the changing international system', in A. Williams and C. Bakir (eds), *Turkey and Europe*, Pinter Publishers, London, 1993, pp. 24–44.

the EC was aggravated by the opening of accession negotiations with Greece, with which Turkey was engaged in a series of bilateral disputes in the Aegean. The Turkish government regarded the Greek accession application as 'a political act aimed at getting a new international platform against Turkey'.[2] Rather than seeking closer ties with the EC to balance the Greek factor, the Turkish response was to move away from the relationship. In October 1978 the Ecevit government imposed a unilateral freeze on the Association, reneging on the commitment to proceed to the next round of tariff cuts.

Although the Turkish side rapidly changed its mind and began seriously to consider applying for full membership,[3] the military coup of 12 September 1980 effectively ruled this out. In January 1982 the Association was officially suspended by the EC following a vote in the European Parliament. Even after the Turkish parliamentary elections of 1983 restored a civilian government (with a military president), another three years were to pass before the Association Agreement began to operate again, with an Association Council meeting held at ambassadorial level in 1986. As a result, it was not until 1987 that the Turkish government finally submitted its accession application—12 years after Greece and 10 years after Spain and Portugal.

On the other side, Heinz Kramer notes that 'one can easily come to the conclusion that the EC and its member states did not undertake strong efforts to make the Ankara Agreement and the Additional Protocol a success'.[4] Apart from the textiles issue, he points particularly to the EC's failure to meet its commitment under the Association Agreement to 'progressively securing free movement of workers',[5] to the different interpretations which the two sides had concerning the promised harmonization of agricultural policy, and to the difficulties in ratifying financial aid to Turkey. The Greek Association, which included many similar terms to the Ankara Agreement, faced similar difficulties.

When it came to the Turkish accession application, EC reluctance was even more pronounced. It took over two and a half years before the European Commission issued its *Opinion*. The latter was negative on two grounds. First, the Commission stated that it would be 'unwise' to start new accession negotiations at a time when the Single European Act had only recently come into force and the Community was still digesting the previous Enlargement. Second, it declared that the political and economic situation in Turkey meant that 'it would not be useful to open accession negotiations with Turkey straight away'. Instead, it put off all discussion of Enlargement until 1993 'at the earliest'.

When 1993 came, the European Union began negotiations with the four EFTA states, Austria, Finland, Norway and Sweden, while encouraging Turkey to apply for completion of the customs union envisaged under the Association as a first major step towards closer relations. By the time the customs union agreement was finalized in 1995, eight Central and East European states (CEECs)

---

[2]*The Economist*, 21 June 1975.

[3]Apparently in June 1980, the Foreign Minister announced that Turkey was planning to submit an application for full membership. M. Müftuler-Bac, *Turkey's Relations with a Changing Europe*, Manchester University Press, Manchester and New York, p. 62.

[4]H. Kramer, 'Turkey and the European Union: A multi-dimensional relationship with hazy perspectives', in V. Mastny and R. C. Nation (eds), *Turkey Between East and West: New Challenges for a Regional Power*, Westview, Boulder CO and Oxford, 1996, pp. 203–232.

[5]Article 12 of the Association Agreement.

had applications on the table, joining Cyprus and Malta which had applied in 1990. At the Luxembourg summit in 1997, at which the European Council decided to open negotiations with selected applicants, Turkey was not even recognized as a candidate but simply declared 'eligible for membership'. It was not until Helsinki in 1999, 12 years after the Turkish government had submitted its application, that Turkey was accorded official candidate status. Another five years were to pass before negotiations began, by which time the Fifth Enlargement had already brought Cyprus, Malta and eight CEECs into the EU.

Turkey's entry talks are expected to be singularly long and hard; already, leading EU politicians have suggested that they may not end in full EU membership. A major obstacle to Turkish accession is clearly the EU's capacity to integrate Turkey. This is a multi-faceted problem, presupposing a major overhaul of the EU's institutional structures, major policies and budget. Essentially, an EU which has prepared to integrate Turkey is likely to be a rather different entity from the Union which we know today. However, the changes that will be required on the part of the EU are only one side of the story. The other concerns the changes that will be required from Turkey.

Redefining Turkey

Looking back to 1963, it is clear that while the Ankara Agreement had foreseen eventual full Turkish membership, this had always been envisaged in a rather long term perspective. Entry would take place at some indefinite future date following the completion of the customs union. But with the passage of time and the evolution of the integration process, the rules of the Enlargement game changed. In the era when the Ankara Agreement was signed, the only criterion specified for applicant countries was that they should be 'European'.[6] At the official ceremony to sign the Turkish Association, European Commission President Walter Hallstein unequivocally declared Turkey to be part of Europe. Subsequently, there has been much less certainty about this.

Turkey's strategic significance during the Cold War had encouraged its definition as 'European', facilitating its admission to such European entities as the Organization for European Economic Coordination and the Council of Europe, as well as its Association with the EC and the eventual membership prospect that it was offered in the early 1960s. But since then, the definition of 'European' has shifted, acquiring a strong normative content. In parallel with its continual economic deepening and the acquisition of an ever broader public policy remit, the European integration project has, since at least the early 1970s, sought to develop a collective identity based on shared civilisational values. Central to this has been what has been described as the 'democratic tradition' of European integration: an image of the EC\EU and its member-states as the repository of a historic tradition of devotion to democracy.[7] Perhaps the classic expression of this idea was the Laeken Declaration of December 2001, which

---

[6]Article 237 of the Treaty of Rome.

[7]The point of course is not the extent to which this image corresponds with the reality of recent European history, but the role which it has played in identity-building within the EC\EU. S. Verney, 'Creating the democratic tradition of European integration: the South European catalyst', in H. Sjursen (ed.), *Enlargement and the Finality of the EU*, Oslo, Arena, 2002, pp. 97–127.

proclaimed Europe to be 'the continent of humane values, the Magna Carta, the Bill of Rights, the French Revolution and the fall of the Berlin Wall', with its 'one boundary' being 'democracy and human rights'.[8]

This 'democratic tradition' has found concrete expression in the growing emphasis on democracy as a criterion for membership, initially proposed by the European Parliament in 1962, first put into practice with the sanctions imposed on the dictatorships in Greece in 1967 and Turkey in 1982, and formally consolidated with the official entry criteria established at Copenhagen in 1993. Subsequently, adherence to democratic standards has been prioritized over all other criteria for EU membership. Thus, states are required sufficiently to meet the political criteria before opening entry negotiations. In contrast, the other criteria—even that of a fully functioning market economy—only need to be fulfilled before accession. This prioritization reflects the fact that democracy is more than a formal entry requirement: it has come to be regarded as a fundamental proof of a state's European identity.

With the growing emphasis on democracy as the primary defining characteristic of a European state, Turkey's classification in this category came increasingly into question. Turkey's image has not corresponded with the democratic European ideal. The country's relations with the EC were set back three times by military coups, in 1960, 1971 and 1980. Then, just a decade ago, in 1997, in an era when Turkey was actively seeking EU membership, a 'postmodern' military intervention, not involving bloodshed, led to the fall of an Islamist government opposed by the military. At other periods the military has continued to play an influential role in politics, which has been institutionalized through its participation in the National Security Council. This is clearly not compatible with contemporary West European expectations of civilian control over the military and the latter's absence from political life. At the same time, there has been a constant stream of international criticism concerning inadequate respect of human and minority rights and fundamental political freedoms in Turkey.

Then in the 1980s a new element was added to the picture. The growing international concern with the rise of Islamic fundamentalism across a broad geographic region encompassing Central Asia, the Middle East and north Africa,[9] began to influence perceptions of Turkey. Even before Samuel Huntington formulated his famous 'clash of civilisations' thesis,[10] the fact that Turkish society is predominantly Muslim gained a new and negative prominence in discussion of Turkey's relations with the EC. The result was a much stronger emphasis on Turkey as culturally 'Other'. This included a focus on the historical past—particularly the Ottoman past with images of the Turks hammering on the gates of Vienna—rather than on the postwar political constellation which had led to Turkey's recognition as part of 'Europe'. Inevitably, the approaching end of the

---

[8] 'The future of the European Union', Declaration of the European Council, Laeken, 15 December 2001, available at www.consilium.europa.eu.

[9] For just two examples of the abundant academic literature on this theme, see Y. M. Choueiri, *Islamic Fundamentalism*, Frances Pinter, London, 1990 and J. L. Esposito, *The Islamic Threat: Myth or Reality*, Oxford University Press, New York and Oxford, 1992.

[10] S. P. Huntington, 'The Clash of Civilisations?', *Foreign Affairs*, Vol 72, No 3, Summer 1993, pp. 22–49 and *The Clash of Civilisations and the Remaking of World Order*, Simon & Schuster, New York, 1996.

Cold War downgraded the importance of the immediate postwar view of Turkey as 'European'. Instead, there was a new focus on the country's relations with the Middle East, which in turn reinforced the emphasis on the country's Muslim identity.

For many Europeans, a key element of the latter concerns gender roles. The issue of the headscarf has proved particularly potent in West European perceptions, serving as the symbolic expression of a disadvantaged role for women in Islamic society. Particularly through the issues of the rights of women and minorities, Turkish identity has, in the minds of many Europeans, become negatively linked with democracy and human rights. Meanwhile, after the attacks on the World Trade Centre on 11 September 2001 and particularly after the London bombings of July 2005, an additional negative ingredient has been the association so frequently made between terrorism and Islam.

Thus, a key issue for Turkey on its road to the European Union is how to change the country's image, so that its national identity is seen as compatible with European ideas of democracy and rights—and hence of European identity. Like all post-1993 applicants for EU entry, Turkey has to conform to the political criteria of Copenhagen,[11] with its compliance subject to European Commission surveillance and recorded in annual monitoring reports. But in the Turkish case, it will not be sufficient to convince European Commission officials that political change has been substantive. It will also be necessary to persuade a broader European public that the Turkish reality does not correspond to the prevailing stereotypes.

While in the case of previous Enlargements, the debate was essentially contained as a narrow discourse among strong publics, the Turkish candidacy has already become the subject of broader public discussion. The controversy around the Turkish case has occurred in the context of the developing debate on the EU's democratic legitimacy. The latter, having entered a new phase after the Maastricht referendums in 1992, gained further impetus with the 2005 Constitutional Treaty debacle. The Chirac legacy—the new French condition that all future EU Enlargement be endorsed by a national referendum—means that at the end of the accession negotiations, it will be necessary for the French public, at least, to be convinced to vote for Turkish entry. And the French constitutional requirement may be only the first step in the opening up of the EU Enlargement process to a broader range of veto players. Even if the public in other member-states is not given a direct opportunity to endorse Turkish accession, it seems likely that negative public opinion will influence national decision-makers, particularly now that the elitist character of the integration project has become so clearly contested.

And in the case of Enlargement to Turkey, public opinion to date has indeed been negative. The autumn 2006 *Eurobarometer* survey found that while 46% of respondents across the EU supported further Enlargement, only 28% thought the EU should admit Turkey while 59% were against.[12] In a study based on *Eurobarometer* data, A. Ruiz-Jiménez and J. I. Torreblanca found that opposition

---

[11]'Stability of institutions guaranteeing democracy, the rule of law, human rights and respect for and protection of minorities.'

[12]*Eurobarometer 66: Public Opinion in the European Union*, 2007, European Commission: Directorate General Communication, available at http://ec.europa.eu/public_opinion, pp. 218, 223.

to Turkish membership was mainly connected with identity-related arguments. As they noted, 'the more the identity dimension figures in public debate and attitudes towards Turkey, the more probable it is that support will be low'.[13] Strikingly, in the autumn 2006 *EB*, almost two-thirds of respondents (61%) felt the cultural differences between Turkey and the EU to be too significant to allow for accession. Meanwhile, an overwhelming majority (85%) felt that Turkey's accession should be dependent on its systematic respect for human rights.[14]

The challenge for the next Turkish governments is therefore immense. Achieving EU entry will require nothing less than a reclassification of Turkey to fit the contemporary definition of 'European'. This presupposes a radical shift in external perceptions of the country's national identity, with Turkey acquiring a 'European' image as a democratic state with full respect for rights. A central element of this image shift will be to prove that Islam and democracy can be compatible. If this can be done, even if Turkey's accession process suffers a setback—due, for example, to the opposition of the current French President or any other EU politician—it will become very hard for the EU and its member-states to justify keeping Turkey outside the EU indefinitely. Such an argument would lack moral legitimacy. Excluding a candidate which had met all the membership criteria and fully established its credentials as a European state— especially if it had passed through a long process of negotiation and monitoring in order to do so—would dramatically damage the credibility of the Union, not to mention that of any future Enlargement prospect.

Political change and national identity

It is for this reason that this special issue has focused on the questions of national identity and political change: because these are considered the key to the success or failure of the Turkish integration project. The first four articles in this collection focus on the process of domestic reform, which began after the Helsinki decision to recognise Turkey as a candidate in 1999 and gained major momentum with the election of the AKP government in 2002.

Kostas Ifantis, outlining the context in which the process of political change in Turkey is unfolding, describes the present juncture as 'a time of peril'. Externally, almost two decades after the end of the Cold War, the relationship between Turkey and the West still lacks a sense of direction. Meanwhile, the shifting regional balance, of which the war in Iraq is just one aspect, contains inherent threats to Turkish security. Domestically, with the election of the AKP in 2002, the country appears to have broken out of the cycle of internally divided coalition governments and entered a modernising phase, marked by progress in political reform and impressive economic growth. However, the success of the moderate Islamist AKP has challenged the power of traditional secular elites. At the same time, integration into the 'sovereignty-diluting' EU is undermining Turkish traditions of strong state sovereignty. This has triggered a nationalist reaction, aiming to annul the reform process and finding violent expression in the

---

[13]A. Ruiz-Jiménez and J. I. Torreblanca, *European Public Opinion and Turkey's Accession: Making Sense of Arguments For and Against*, European Policy Institutes Network, Working Paper No. 16, May 2007, p. 11.

[14]*Eurobarometer 66*, op.cit., pp. 224–5.

assassination of Turkish-Armenian journalist, Hrant Dink. The outcome has been a dangerous polarisation between Islamist and secular forces, manifested in the spring 2007 presidential election crisis and taking place in a climate of rising euroscepticism.

Tracing the course of Turkish domestic reform since 1995, Luigi Narbone and Nathalie Tocci argue that this has been a cyclical process, which has paralleled the 'ebbs and flows' in Turkish-EU relations. While recognising that other internal and external factors provide the principal explanation for Turkey's domestic transformation, they show that whenever the EU has responded positively to Turkey's approaches, this has strengthened the domestic pro-reform coalition. Thus, the Helsinki decision to accept Turkey as a candidate in 1999 opened a 'virtuous' cycle, catalyzing a phase of unprecedented domestic reform. In contrast, whenever the EU has appeared to turn away from Turkey, this has strengthened the nationalist opponents of reform, threatening to draw the reform process into a new 'vicious' cycle. A key factor in permitting political liberalization has been the reduced perception of an Islamist threat, as a result of the channeling of Islamist protest through the AKP and the latter's evolution into a mainstream political party. This has reduced the power of the traditional security narrative, which had been a major factor inhibiting democratisation. While the AKP after 2002 emerged as an important agent of the reforms sought by the EU, the authors note that its continued support for the project of democratic change cannot be taken for granted. They conclude that EU support will be essential if the point of irreversibility in domestic reform is to be reached.

Addressing the apparent paradox of Turkey's europeanising Islamists, Ziya Önis argues that Turkish politics since 1999 cannot be understood on the basis of the traditional left-right axis. Instead, the predominant cleavage is that between 'conservative globalists', promoting the domestic reform process, and 'defensive nationalists', resisting it. Many of the secular elites, including the military, which have traditionally supported westernisation, are uncomfortable with the political reforms promoted through EU conditionality. While they would support EU entry if this did not entail reform, the author points out that it is meaningless to talk about one in the absence of the other. In contrast, the moderate Islamists of the AKP have become the most vigorous elements of the globalising pro-reform coalition, being transformed in the process into self-processed 'Muslim democrats'. However, since 2005, the AKP has been on the defensive and has apparently lost its reformist zeal. This has been due to the nationalist reaction, to the rising euroscepticism partially fuelled by the negative intra-EU debate preceding the opening of accession negotiations, to disillusion with EU policy towards northern Cyprus, and to the disappointment of its core constituency with the EU's failure to promote religious freedoms in Turkey. The author therefore suggests there may be structural limits to the role of a conservative, religious-based party in promoting the Europeanisation agenda. However, there is no credible agent of Europeanisation on the centre-left, as the main party in this area of the political spectrum, the CHP, is characterised by soft euroscepticism and resistance to reform. The author argues that the absence of a major European-style social democratic party represents a major weakness for Turkey's accession process: both domestically, in order to promote democratisation and externally, given that European social democrats constitute a major source of support for Turkish membership.

Continuing the theme of Europeanisation, Mustafa Aydin and Sinem Acikmese examine how the accession process and EU conditionality have operated in one particular sphere: that of Turkish foreign policy, where there has been considerable change over the past decade. Interpreting Europeanisation as a 'top-down' process, they examine three different conditionality mechanisms. Compliance with the Copenhagen criteria has resulted in reforms of the National Security Council, reducing the comparative weight of the military and paving the way for a civilianised foreign policy. Compliance with the 'good neighbourliness' criterion adopted at Helsinki in 1999 has played a significant role in both the post-1999 Greek-Turkish rapprochement and the subsequent switch in Cyprus policy towards support for the search for a solution in the context of the Annan Plan. In contrast, alignment with the Common Foreign and Security Policy *acquis* has been only one of the factors explaining changes in Turkish policy towards the Middle East.

The next two papers are concerned with issues of national identity and directly address aspects of the negative image associated with Islam. The attack on the World Trade Centre has triggered a debate on the role played by religiosity—and Islam in particular—in precipitating acts of political protest and violence. So far, however, the debate has focused on the role of Islamic beliefs in nurturing protest in non-Muslim societies. In an important empirical study, based on over 2,000 interviews conducted in 33 Turkish provinces, Ersin Kalaycioğlu investigates the linkage between religiosity and protest in the predominantly Sunni Muslim society of Turkey. He draws the conclusion that protest acts are often the resort of 'desperate souls', a category to which the religious orders, which tend to be well integrated into the political and economic system, do not usually belong. Moreover, he points out that Sunni Islam does not condone protest acts, which appear to be perceived as rebellious behaviour. He concludes that in the context of the overwhelmingly Sunni Muslim society of Turkey, religiosity does indeed influence protest behaviour—but by forestalling rather than fostering it.

Meanwhile, in a first report on a long-term research project, based on the study of parliamentary debates, websites, secondary sources and elite inter-views, Hakan Yilmaz deconstructs the image of Turkey as 'the Other' in the discourse of French and German opponents of Turkish accession. The basic argument concerns Turkish 'cultural incompatibility' with Europe. Central to the latter is the role of Christianity, seen not as a theological system but as a civilisational idea, whose values are believed to provide the very essence of European identity. In contrast, Turkey is clearly equated with Islam, whose negative image is strongly based on its perceived association with sexual and political violence. In particular, the headscarf, symbolising women's submission to men, signals a culture dominated by an uncontrolled male psyche, the antithesis of a European civilisation which has re-channelled male energy to peaceful and productive ends. The author concludes that a new Turkish focus on 'Enlightenment values' might be the best way to counter these perceptions.

Susannah Verney considers the problems of the Turkish accession negotiations in the light of previous Enlargement experience. She shows that the EU has habitually been a reluctant party to entry talks. However, the cost for individual member-states of saying 'no' to specific candidates has resulted in a 'default drive' dynamic of accepting the opening of accession negotiations.

Subsequently, the fact that some governments may be opposed to Enlargement, combined with a more general tendency to defer difficult decisions until later, has encouraged a preference for postponement, even in the case of candidates considerably less challenging than Turkey. This leaves the onus for success on the candidate. Based on the experience of successful past entrants, the author suggests a negotiating strategy which combines flexibility in the technical entry talks with two further ingredients. Both speak directly to the special issue's themes of national identity and political change. The first is the importance for the national image of having 'a man we can trust'—preferably an individual who symbolizes the national struggle for democracy—as leader of the government and central interlocutor of the EU partners. The second is the employment of a norm-driven rhetorical strategy, presenting accession as a moral imperative due to its role as a lever and stabilizer of democratic change. She recommends that the Turkish government claim a modern 'European' identity for Turkey, based on adherence to the European values of democracy and European integration—a strategy which, of course, presupposes that future Turkish governments will demonstrate in practice their devotion to these ideals.

All the preceding articles were initially published as a special issue of the *Journal of Southern Europe and the Balkans*. For the book, a final chapter by Kıvanç Ulusoy and Susannah Verney has been added on the key topic of Turkey's Cyprus policy. The latter was considered to merit special examination, both because of its role as a marker of national identity and political change in the first decade of the 21st century and because of the significance of the Cyprus conflict as a structural obstacle to Turkish accession. The examination of this topic is framed in the context of 'democratic peace theory' and focuses on the inter-linkage between Europeanisation, democratisation and changing Cyprus policy. The study illustrates the EC\EU's lack of impact on Turkey's Cyprus policy for decades, until it made a commitment to ultimate Turkish membership, and then shows how change in Cyprus policy occurred under a pro-reform government operating in the context of EU conditionality. However, in a third phase post-2004, the new impasse in Cyprus policy following the failed Annan Plan referenda resulted in negative feedback into the domestic democratisation process, in turn limiting the possibilities for 'democratic peace'. The article underlines the significance of credible EU commitments for domestic and foreign policy change in Turkey. It concludes by stressing the crucial significance of a renewed alliance between the EU and domestic reformers for Turkey's European future.

Turkey in transition—opportunities amidst peril?

KOSTAS IFANTIS

On 3 October 2005, Turkey's bid to join the European Union turned a corner with the opening of accession negotiations. The terms of accession and Turkey's long-term prospects for EU membership, however, remain rather unclear. The need to better understand the factors that will shape the course of EU–Turkey relations is critical.

Turkey's accession talks have already put Ankara's bid, as well as the EU's role and identity, into a new perspective. To become a member, Turkey must meet all the criteria and requirements laid out in the Negotiating Framework adopted in September 2005. On the political level, Turkey must create stable institutions that guarantee democracy, the rule of law, human rights and respect for minorities. It should also unequivocally commit itself to good neighbourly relations and to the peaceful solution of border disputes according to the UN Charter and international law. Economically, the EU expects Turkey to create a functioning market economy and to adopt the acquis communautaire. All these will require Turkey to reform itself drastically to adopt, implement and enforce the European principles and values.

However, the accession talks are taking place against a backdrop of a very sceptical EU public opinion as well as an elite majority that is less tolerant towards Turkey's European prospects. Old prejudices against Turkey, mainly based on religion and history, are still very present and they are reinforced by more pragmatic concerns, related to the basic arithmetics of the EU functioning: number of votes in the Council, European Parliament seats, funding and subsidies, etc. And it is true that the thorniest issue in the whole process is the EU's capacity to absorb Turkey. Financially, Turkey's integration can only happen after an overhaul of the EU's budget and redistribution mechanisms. The institutional changes required must be fundamental.

All the above is the reason why Turkey negotiates its European future under the most stringent terms any candidate ever had to endure in the history of European integration and that is why to have any chance for success, Turkey will have to win the hearts and minds of EU citizens,[1] and this must be done by a country at a time of peril.

The end of the cold war and the end of domestic certainties

For Turkey, the collapse of the USSR 'has had enormous adverse repercussions on an entirely different front: cohesion in the western world. For Ankara, this has meant less confidence in the willingness and ability of major NATO allies

---

[1]Burak Akcapar and Denis Chaibi, 'Turkey's EU accession: the long road from Ankara to Brussels', *Yale Journal of International Affairs*, Winter/Spring 2006, p. 53.

to continue business as usual with Turkey.'[2] Developments in the East outpaced whatever meagre prospects Turkey might have enjoyed in Western European eyes.[3] America's traditionally strong military relationship with Turkey was called into question, economic and military assistance programmes were reduced and eventually zeroed out. Even cash purchases of arms and equipment became subject to US congressional holds. In short, the changing geopolitical environment in the late 1980s and early 1990s presented Turkey with many new challenges. These included a fragmentation of power along its northern and north-eastern borders following the strategic withdrawal of Soviet/Russian power; the multiplication of political actors in the wider Eurasian region; the emergence and, in some cases, intensification of, local conflicts with the potential to escalate into larger regional conflicts; and the absence of an easily conceived and articulated threat, 'further isolating Turkey from mainstream European political and economic developments'.[4]

At that time, the quest for a new role, that of peacemaker and regional stabilizer, began. President Özal went on to define Turkey as a model for the region because of its unique combination of characteristics: Islamic, democratic, secular and, above all, stable in the midst of a disintegrating region ranging from the Balkans, to the former USSR, to the Middle East. The Gulf War I simply revalidated Turkey's self-definition and role in this context. Security debates in the USA and Europe acknowledged Turkey's geopolitical significance and the need to reinvigorate relations with Ankara. But there was relatively little substance in defining what a new agenda for strategic cooperation between Turkey and the West should have included.

Fifteen years later, it seems that the relationship between Turkey and the West still lacks a clear sense of direction. Uncertainty remains as to what big issues parties can work for, or against, in a new strategic environment. Special reference must be made to the concept of Turkey as a 'pivotal state'. Turkey fulfils all the requirements of a pivotal state: population, location, and economic and military potential. Its defining quality, though, is the potential to affect regional and international stability. Turkey's significance lies not only in its geostrategic value, but also in the destabilization and uncertainty that the (even remote) possibility of its decline might result in.[5]

The regional balance, and for that reason, the geostrategic value and role of Turkey, will continue to depend on a number of factors, which seemingly contribute—albeit unevenly—to either enhancing or diminishing Turkey's role in regional and world politics, in the framework of US and European foreign policy and security interests. The most important of these factors is Turkey's relations with the USA and its position in the wider American security strategic plan, shaped by the future development of: (1) relations between the USA/West and Iraq (and Iran) especially after the 2003 campaign against Baghdad and the occupation of Iraq; (2) relations between the West and Russia as well as the

---

[2]Duygu B. Sezer, 'Turkey in the new security environment in the Balkan and Black Sea region', in Vojtech Mastny and R. Craig Nation (eds), *Turkey Between East and West: New Challenges for a Rising Regional Power*, Westview, Boulder, CO, 1996, p. 74.

[3]Ibid.

[4]Ibid., pp. 74–75.

[5]Robert Chase, Emily Hill and Paul Kennedy, 'Pivotal states and US strategy', *Foreign Affairs*, 75(1), January–February 1996, pp. 33–51.

general foreign and security policy goals of Moscow; (3) Turkish–Russian relations, especially in the strategic environment of the Caucasus and Central Asia. It will also be subject to: (4) continuation and intensification of the conventional arms race in the region and the horrifying prospect of weapons of mass destruction (WMD) proliferation; (5) the stability prospects of Central Asian countries and the security of the oil routes; (6) the future of the EU–Turkish relationship and the prospects of membership. Finally, (7) the issue of Turkish national power itself, with reference to not only the military dimension, but mainly to the political, economic and social development of the country. The last two factors are of critical importance and are directly linked to the management of internal political, economic and social uncertainties.

In this context, Turkish society, politics and economy have evolved substantially since the early 1990s. The pace of this change has increased in recent years, and has included the rise of a much wider and more active debate on all aspects of public policy and socio-political development. The period since 1999 can been seen as 'the formative years' of a new domestic landscape, where the drive for modernization seems to be reshaping traditional perceptions and Manichaeist principles of socio-political formation.

The 1999 general elections produced a nationalist coalition of the right and the left, with a sharp decline in support for centrist parties and for the Islamic political agents. The consolidation of military influence in defence of the secular state, which began with the removal of the Welfare Party (*Refah Partisi*—RP) from power and its banning from Turkish politics, also meant that the Turkish military remains a key interlocutor in foreign and security policy issues.[6] Three years later, the Turkish general election of 3 November 2002, transformed the country's political landscape dramatically. None of the members of the outgoing governing coalition won seats in the new parliament. Since taking office in 1999, the coalition had been tarnished by a series of corruption scandals. Additionally, during its time in office, the country experienced the worst economic recession in 50 years.[7] The Justice and Development Party (*Adalet ve Kalkınma Partisi*—AKP), formed in mid-2001, came to power with 34.3 per cent of the vote and a massive majority of 363 seats in the 550-member parliament. The centre-left Republican People's Party (*Cumhuriyet Halk Partisi*—CHP), after its disastrous performance in the 1999 election, emerged as the second party with 19.4 per cent of the vote and 178 seats. Another nine seats were won by independents with all other political parties failing to cross the 10 per cent threshold.[8]

The indications of transition turbulence were strong. A transition that culminated in a crisis with the powerful Turkish military, backed by the secular

(margin annotation, left side: Political reformation)

---

[6]Ibid., p. 28.

[7]During 2001, the Turkish economy contracted by 9.4 per cent, resulting in over a million redundancies and forcing the government to agree to a painful IMF-sponsored economic stabilization programme.

[8]The three parties in the coalition government saw their total vote fall to 14.7 per cent from 53.4 per cent in 1999. Additionally, the opposition leaders were voted out. Tansu Ciller's True Path Party (*Doğru Yol Partisi*—DYP) won just 9.6 per cent of the vote as compared to 12 per cent in 1999. See Gareth Jenkins, 'Muslim democrats in Turkey?', *Survival*, 45(1), Spring 2003, pp. 54–55. For further details, see Ali Carkoglu, 'The rise of the new generation pro-Islamists in Turkey: the Justice and Development Party phenomenon in the November 2002 elections in Turkey', *South European Society and Politics*, 7(1), 2003.

establishment, over who should be the country's next President, led to the early elections of 22 July 2007. The AKP was returned to office after it won a landslide victory. The elections were marked by an 84 per cent turnout when a record high 42.5 million voters cast ballots. Out of 550 parliamentary seats, 341 went to the ruling party, 112 to the CHP, 71 to the far-right Nationalist Action Party (MHP) and 26 to the independents, most of whom are Kurds. The AKP increased its share of the national vote from 34.3 to 46.7 per cent. The CHP, which campaigned on the threat to secularism, won 20.9 per cent of the vote, while the MHP won 14.3 per cent.[9]

The AKP won in all but a few coastal provinces in the west. Even in traditional bastions of Kemalism, like Izmir, the CHP narrowly escaped defeat, while in Antalya, the home province of CHP leader Deniz Baykal, the AKP won. In the predominantly Kurdish south-east, the ruling party doubled its share from roughly 26 per cent in 2002 to 53 per cent in 2007. The CHP, despite its merger with the Democratic Left Party, fared well only in some western provinces while it fell below 10 per cent in the south-east. The MHP succeeded in doubling its vote, doing especially well in western and southern Turkey. Undoubtedly, the MHP benefited from the rise of nationalism in Turkey stemming from disenchantment with the long drawn out process of joining the EU, increasing opposition to Turkish membership from countries such as France and the resurgence of terrorism by the Kurdistan Workers Party (PKK).

According to Kerem Oktem, the AKP has succeeded in establishing itself in the societal centre. Moreover, it has now emerged as the only political party that enjoys strong backing across Turkey, and can have a legitimate claim in the representation of both Turks and Kurds, a substantial proportion of the Sunni Alevi community and virtually all social classes.[10] At the same time, the CHP— the oldest Turkish political party, whose logo consists of the six arrows which represent the foundational principles of Kemalist ideology: republicanism, nationalism, statism, populism, secularism and revolutionism—has by all means ceased to be a national party that enjoys support across regional and ethnic divide. Instead, it has become 'a regional party rooted in Turkish identity politics'.[11]

The new parliament is much more representative of the country's complex make-up than the previous one, which had only two parties because of the infamous 10 per cent threshold designed to keep overtly Kurdish parties out of parliament. The presence in parliament of Kurdish deputies and the ultra-nationalist MHP (whose Grey Wolves faction was partly responsible for the escalation of political violence in the 1970s before the 1980 coup) could be an explosive mix.[12] Moreover, though, the results of the 2007 elections indicate that patrician loyalty to modernization as a top-down process 'has outlived the ability to impose such a Jacobin trajectory'. What is emerging is a country 'less beholden

---

[9]Kerem Oktem, 'Harbingers of Turkey's Second Republic', *Middle East Report Online*, 1 August 2007, p. 2, <http://www.merip.org/mero/mero080107.html>.

[10]Surveys show that around half of the voters in the lower- and middle-income groups supported the AKP, while around 35 per cent of upper-middle class and 23 per cent of upper-income groups did likewise. See ibid.

[11]Ibid.

[12]William Chislett, 'Turkey's election: Islamists deal a blow to the secular establishment', Europe—ARI 86/2007, *Real Instituto Elcano*, 24 July 2007, p. 2.

to the military–civilian elite that drove modernization from above, but is more diverse, more inclusive and, dare one say it, more modern'.[13]

Transition?

Until the arrival of the AKP government in 2002, Turkey suffered from a long series of inept and squabbling coalition governments which did very little to modernize the country economically, socially and politically. The AKP is the most successful party in the history of Turkish politics. Its reform record is unprecedented. On the economic front, inflation has been tamed, average per capita income almost doubled between 2003 and 2006 and foreign direct investment has poured in after years of stagnation, stock markets have been rising and trust in the Turkish lira, so badly hit by the financial crisis of 2001, has been restored. On the social and political front, although the pace of reform has not been impressive, human rights and freedom of the press have improved. More importantly, though, the past five years have revealed a very interesting trajectory of the evolution of political Islam in Turkey and the friction between secular and religious outlooks within Turkish society.

Over the past decade, key elements of the Kemalist tradition that guided Turkish perceptions and policies since the foundation of the Republic—secularism, etatism and Western orientation—have come under severe strain. This was particularly evident in the events that led to the 22 July general election. Two aspects of domestic change are particularly important: the rise of Turkish nationalism and the polarization of 'secular' and 'religious' elements in Turkish society.

As far as nationalism is concerned, a strong sense of it has always been imbedded within the Kemalist culture, and has traditionally related to the process of modernization and Westernization of Turkey. The fundamental assumptions underpinning Kemalism have been widely shared among Turkish elites. However, a more vigorous nationalist sentiment has been visible in the Turkish society and body politic since the end of the Cold War. The emergence of independent Turkic republics in Central Asia and the Caucasus stimulated a lively debate in Turkey over the prospects for new ties based on ethnic affinity. This pan-Turkist potential was taken up by elements of the nationalist right and was embraced in a milder form by mainstream parties as well as Turkey's active business community.[14] At the same time, the violent Kurdish insurgency in south-eastern Turkey, led by the PKK, and a more general rise in Kurdish political activism provoked a nationalist reaction across the political spectrum.

This reaction continues today and the nationalist impulse has been reinforced by the post-Iraq War experience and the very uncomforting prospects of an autonomous Kurdish state/province in Northern Iraq backed by the USA. This has fuelled strong anti-American sentiment among the Turkish public, who feel betrayed by the USA. Turkish analysts often refer to the 'Sèvres syndrome', or fear of containment and dismemberment harking back to the 1920 Treaty

---

[13]Oktem (2007), op. cit.

[14]Zalmay Khalilzad, Ian O. Lessr and F. Stephen Larrabee, *The Future of Turkish–Western Relations: Toward a Strategic Plan*, RAND, Santa Barbra, CA, 2000, p. 2.

of Sèvres that began the partition of the Ottoman Empire. Even in moderate circles, this residual concern encourages the view that without considerable vigilance, Turkish sovereignty and national interests may be 'sold out', even by strategic partners in the West. Northern Iraq, closely tied to Kurdish separatism, is the most sensitive example. Ankara has signalled that it could take unilateral military action against the PKK inside Northern Iraq if necessary, and in this framework Turkish troops have been deployed across the Iraqi/Turkish border. Both the USA and the EU remain firmly opposed to any such action. Washington has made it clear that it sees a military solution of the PKK problem inside Iraq as the last resort. This reflects the US reluctance to risk destabilizing the most stable region inside Iraq, where it has a long-time alliance with Kurdish leaders and when the situation in the rest of the country has been constantly deteriorating.[15]

At the same time, flux in Turkey's relations with the EU and the stalling of the EU accession talks process in December 2006 have been contributing to the rise of nationalism. Although the AKP was able to establish a national consensus around EU accession with a high level of support among the population, public opinion began to shift as Turkey entered the accession negotiations phase in 2005, for a number of reasons. Firstly, the anti-Turkish mood in many European quarters expressed in the continued talk of a 'privileged membership' as an alternative to full membership, open-ended talks or eventual 'safeguard clauses' came as a shock to many Turks.

Secondly, the European perspective has not so far resolved Turkey's basic nationalist dilemma. A Turkish elite and public that have grown accustomed to a more vigorous assertion of Turkish nationalism—often in opposition to European preferences—found themselves facing an enormous challenge. Never before have Turkish elites had to confront the dilemma posed by a strong nationalist tradition and a powerful attachment to state sovereignty, on the one hand, with the prospect of integration in a sovereignty-diluting EU, on the other. Even short of full membership, candidacy implies great institutionalized scrutiny, convergence and compromise. From the least political issues (e.g. food regulations) to high politics, a closer relationship with formal EU structures will put tremendous pressure on traditional Turkish concepts of sovereignty at many levels and will severely question (as it has already done) the role of the military in Turkish politics. It is a process that has been difficult for all member states of the EU, though surrendering sovereignty has also been one of the most fundamental elements of European integration success. For an EU member state, pursuing nationalist options outside the integration context has become extremely difficult and costly.

Both issues have contributed to declining public support for the accession process. Nationalists in Turkey have been quick to capitalize on this growing public disenchantment with the EU, and some political parties which previously saw EU membership as a crucial part of Turkey's democratisation and modernization development have joined the eurosceptic camp. The national consensus has been fading away, with every reform being portrayed as a concession to an insincere, hostile, not-to-be-trusted Europe.

---

[15]Amanda Akçakoca, 'EU–Turkey relations 43 years on: train crash or temporary derailment?', European Policy Centre, Issue Paper No. 50, November 2006, available at http://www.epc.eu, p. 24.

At a public discourse level, the nationalist reaction was carried forward by a coalition of anti-liberal forces, made up of retired generals and their civil society organizations, parts of the security services and far-right groups. Between 2005 and 2007 this coalition brought about a climate of fear, aiming at convincing Turks that the political reform process would have to be abandoned.[16] The nationalist counter-movement was not confined to symbolic politics, but expressed itself violently with assassinations—most notably the murder of Turkish-Armenian journalist and activist Hrant Dink in January 2007—and mob attacks. Parallel to that, a wave of prosecutions was mounted against public intellectuals, such as Orhan Pamuk, Elif Shafak, Ragip Zarakolu, Baskin Oran to cite but a few.

With the CHP leader, Deniz Baykal, resorting to an anti-EU, anti-USA and anti-globalization discourse, the nationalist counter-movement soon turned to an old 'trademark' of political polarization in Turkey: the struggle between Islamic forces and the secular tradition of the state. The events that followed in the first six months of 2007 and led to the early elections of 22 July are well known. Following the nomination of Foreign Minister Abdullah Gul as president, a political and constitutional crisis erupted. On 27 April the military issued a statement through their official website, to the effect that 'radical Islamic understanding ... has been expanding its sphere with encouragement from politicians and local authorities ... The Turkish armed forces ... are staunch defenders of secularism ... and will display their position and attitudes when it becomes necessary.'[17] The statement, known in the press as the 'e-memorandum' or the 'e-coup', was an overt threat that the swearing-in of a non-secular president would lead to military intervention to save the secular regime. The opposition, led by CHP, boycotted the vote in parliament and then appealed to the Constitutional Court to have the vote annulled because a quorum of two-thirds of parliament's 550 MPs was not present. On 29 April up to 1 million people took to the streets of Istanbul to stage their protest against the government. The court upheld the appeal on 1 May, thereby cancelling the 9 May vote in parliament when only 50 per cent of the vote would have been required, something the AKP was easily assured of.

The crisis showed that although a lot has changed in Turkey in the 2000s, the mindset of the secular establishment has not followed through.[18] This has been also due to some steps taken by the AKP government which have not helped the party's image with secularists: the effort in 2005 to outlaw adultery, attempts by some mayors to create alcohol-free zones, the issue over the *turban* (a specific headscarf that the secular courts regard as a sign of political Islam) and most importantly policies to create loopholes allowing students at the *imam-hatip* schools (IHS) to transfer to academic high schools before graduation, thus granting them preferential treatment in going on to non-theology majors in universities. According to Cagaptay, 'The entry of the HIS graduates into university departments other than theological fields is not only a technical matter

---

[16]Oktem (2007), p. 4.
[17]Soner Cagaptay, 'How will the Turkish military react?', Europe—ARI 80/2007, *Real Instituto Elcano*, 16 July 2007, p. 1.
[18]Chislett (2007), p. 3.

but has led to a fierce internal debate about universal secular education, a pillar of Turkish secularism'[19] and one of Atatürk's fundamental reforms.

The secular elite fears that if the AKP controlled the presidency as well as the parliament and government, the system of checks and balances that guarantees the secular character of the state would disappear.[20] That is why, since 1972 and the entry into parliament of the Islamic National Salvation Party, the secular bloc/military has been constantly intervening with successive bans. Successive bans which have had no effect, though. Indeed, quite the reverse as the 2007 election results show. What the secular establishment failed to comprehend is that Turkey's Islamism is more a movement than a party, and as such has managed to sustain political momentum, despite the bans. As Chislett has noted, 'the AKP is a bottom-up movement which has successfully challenged the authoritarian, centralized top-down paternalism of the political system'.[21] Traditionally, Islamism in Turkey was built on and legitimized by a strong anti-Western attitude. In the late 1990s, however, the AKP realized that they needed the West in order to confront the Kemalist tradition. They acquired systemic legitimacy by engaging in democratic and human rights discourse and began to challenge the secularist elite.[22] At the same time, secularism while the bedrock of the Republic, founded in 1923 by Atatürk, is equated more with Westernization and modernity than with democracy. Kemalism was a state-centred, elite-defined and illiberal modernization project. Secularism and liberal democracy are not viewed by the Kemalist establishment as necessarily complementary, as they are in the West. The military, in particular, in their self-perceived role as the guardians of the secular and unitary state, occupy the paradoxical position of 'safeguarding' democracy while at the same time being the major impediment to Turkey's true democratisation.

At the end of the day, the annulment of the presidential elections shows the severity of a struggle about the power of an old guard that is cemented in the establishment and threatened by the new forces of AKP, whose growing power is leading to the transformation of Turkey's social and political character. The outcome is not easy to predict. However, much will depend on the attitude of the opposition parties and especially of the CHP. So far the party has failed

---

[19]Cagaptay (2007), p. 4. The HIS were established in the 1950s as vocational schools to train *imams* (clerics) and *hatips* (preachers). Later on however, they emerged as an alternative, religious track to secular education as the number of students who enrolled in these schools exceeded the number of *imams* and *hatips* that were needed. As a result, HIS graduates began to overwhelmingly enter universities as public administration and law majors. By the mid-1990s, the schools had become so widespread that in the conflict between the Islamic Rafah Party and the secular establishment in 1997, HIS constituted a point of friction. In the end, secular pressures forced the implementation of new laws stipulating that HIS graduates would be systematically directed to enter universities as theology majors as was originally intended. The barrier stymied the growth of HIS, and the number of students at these schools dropped to 64,534 in 2002. Since the rise of the AKP government however, the number of HIS students has increased. In 2005, 108,064 youths studied at the HIS.

[20]William Chislett, 'Turkey's military throw down the gauntlet', Europe—ARI 51/2007, *Real Instituto Elcano*, 7 May 2007, p. 2. The President, who swears an oath of allegiance to the 'secular nature of the Republic', is Commander-in-Chief of the armed forces, responsible for the appointment of judges, top members of the Administration and university rectors and has a veto power over laws approved by parliament.

[21]Ibid.

[22]Deniz Devrim, 'Blockade of the Turkish presidential elections: a clash of wills between moderate Islamists and the secular establishment', Europe—ARI 59/2007, *Real Instituto Elcano*, 28 May 2007, p. 4.

to stake out a position as a democratic alternative to the AKP, let alone to consolidate itself as a progressive, democratizing force with a European outlook. If it continues the politics of disengagement, coalition with anti-democratic forces and anti-EU and militarist discourses, it risks deteriorating 'into an alliance of inward-looking extreme nationalists, disgruntled former state elites and disoriented upper-middle class voters'.[23] The negative impact on a sustainable democratic process at this critical juncture of Turkish political development cannot be underestimated.

---

[23]Oktem (2007), p. 6.

Running around in circles? The cyclical relationship between Turkey and the European Union

LUIGI NARBONE and NATHALIE TOCCI

Since the establishment of the republic, Turkey's development has evolved in ebbs and flows. Periods of growth, modernization and political liberalization have alternated with years of political instability, violence and economic crisis. Since the late 1990s, these cyclical trends have run parallel to Turkey's relationship with the European Union (EU). Turkey's ties with the Union have been far from linear. While generally moving towards greater levels of integration, relations have been often marred by moments of tension and crisis. The argument developed below is that as Turkey's integration with the EU has proceeded, the ups and downs in EU–Turkey relations have increasingly interacted with Turkey's domestic transformation, at times promoting change while at other times hindering modernization and democratisation. This paper delves into this interaction, exploring how and why the EU dimension has affected the acceleration, deceleration or retreat of Turkey's reform process.

The principal claim made here is that EU relations have acted as a key external factor in Turkey's internal development. This does not mean that the Union has been the principal explanatory variable of Turkey's domestic transformation. Wider international changes and internal factors carry much more weight in determining domestic trends in Turkey. EU relations, however, have been and will continue to represent a fundamental explanatory variable, precisely because of the ways in which they impinge upon domestic factors within Turkey itself. This paper first briefly outlines the chronology of Turkey's turbulent path to Europe and the matching trends in its domestic environment, highlighting how EU relations have impacted upon the process of domestic transformation. It then delves into the endogenous drivers of Turkey's evolution, indicating the principal channels through which these domestic determinants have interacted with the wider setting of EU–Turkey ties.

The long path of EU–Turkey relations

Turkey's first contractual relationship with the then European Economic Community (EEC) dates back to 1963, with the signature of the association agreement. The agreement envisaged the establishment of a customs union and opened the door to accession if and when the political and economic conditions were met. The subsequent decades witnessed a series of ups and downs in EEC–Turkey relations, mainly as a result of Turkey's domestic turmoil. The military coups in 1971 and 1980 and the Turkish military intervention in Cyprus in 1974 magnified tensions with Europe. However, even at the most difficult moments,

Turkey never abandoned its rhetorical goal of moving closer to the Community. In 1987, following gradual domestic stabilization and economic liberalization, Turkey submitted a formal request for membership. But partly because of the Community's internal task of completing the single market and partly because of the problematic state of Turkish democracy and the mounting violence in the south-east, in 1989 Turkey's application was rejected and Turkey's European future was put on hold.

The end of the Cold War brought about radical changes to Turkey's environment. Turkey's role as western sentinel against Soviet expansionism ended, ushering the way to a new period of mounting instability in the Middle East and Eurasia. Turkey consequently underwent an intense period of soul-searching, assessing alternative geostrategic options such as pan-Turkism or regional leadership in the Middle East. Ultimately, the domestic debate converged on a renewed emphasis on the EU project. Turkish political démarchès intensified, lobbying for inclusion in the EU custom union. Meanwhile the nature of European integration was changing, with the Community gradually developing an explicitly political dimension. Since 1978 democracy had been a clear criterion for EC membership, and in the 1986 Single European Act, the required human rights standards within member states were further clarified. The political criteria for entry were fully elaborated at the 1993 European Council in Copenhagen.

The entry into force of the Turkey–EU customs union in January 1996 was the starting point for higher levels of economic integration, and was viewed in Turkey as a prelude to membership. In this context, EU actors became increasingly alert to Turkey's political shortcomings. An important example occurred in 1995 when, following the arrest of several Kurdish deputies, the European Parliament (EP) delayed the ratification of the agreement. While snubbing the pressure for overarching political reforms, Turkey slightly modified a controversial article of its anti-terror law, unblocking the EP's ratification.[1] The link between Turkey's political reforms and EU–Turkey relations was in the offing, opening the way to the EU's growing impact on Turkey's political structures and practices.

The positive atmosphere created by the conclusion of the customs union agreement deteriorated rapidly in 1997. This occurred when the European Council in Luxemburg underlined that Turkey did not meet the standards for candidacy, and offered instead a 'European strategy' based on the exploitation of the integration prospects foreseen under existing contractual relationships. Unlike 1989, this second rejection, together with the EU's finger-pointing at Turkey's deficiencies, was perceived in Ankara as a clear case of discrimination. In response, Turkey froze its political dialogue with the Union, and threatened to withdraw its membership application and integrate with the unrecognized Turkish Cypriot republic. The goal of full membership was not abandoned however, and the Turkish establishment began displaying a dichotomous approach to the Union, which would consolidate in the years ahead. While the government stepped up its campaign to obtain candidacy, the domestic political debate was rife with criticism of the Union. The ensuing 1997–1999 vicious circle in EU–Turkey ties was matched by slow progress in domestic political reforms

---

[1] S. Krauss, 'The European Parliament in EU external relations: the customs union with Turkey', *European Foreign Affairs Review*, 5, 2000, pp. 215–237.

in Turkey. The only steps forward were the minor amendments in the penal code,[2] the reduction of police custody for suspected crimes and the removal of military judges from serving in state security courts (SSCs).

The tide turned with the 1999 Helsinki European Council, when Turkey's long-sought candidacy was recognized. The European Council, however, refrained from opening accession negotiations with Turkey, arguing that the country had first to fulfil the Copenhagen political criteria. In turn, the Commission was given a mandate to monitor progress and to draft a first Accession Partnership for Turkey, recommending areas for reform. The EU also adapted its financial assistance to Turkey, redirecting aid to provide more explicit support for Turkey's reforms. As a result, the interaction between Turkey's domestic evolution and EU–Turkey ties intensified. However, Turkey's steps towards reform were however initially slow and tentative. The first major breakthrough came almost two years after the Helsinki decision, when 34 constitutional articles were amended in October 2001. An even more acute turning point in reform efforts came in August 2002, when parliament approved a far-reaching third legal harmonization package, including the abolition of the death penalty, the right to broadcast and teach in languages other than Turkish, the liberalization of the freedoms of speech, association and assembly, and the recognition of religious minorities' property rights. The acceleration of Turkey's reform momentum spilled over into EU–Turkey relations, especially when the Copenhagen European Council in December 2002 concluded that it would determine whether and when to open accession negotiations with Turkey in December 2004. The approaching green light for the opening of negotiations in turn set the target and the timeline for the new Justice and Development Party (AKP) government elected in November 2002. In fact, 2003 and 2004 were the highest intensity years of the reform process. Another major constitutional reform, five additional legislative packages, a new penal code and numerous laws and regulations modified many of the most restrictive features of Turkey's legal and political system.

As a result, the December 2004 European Council's verdict was that Turkey 'sufficiently' fulfilled the political criteria and that accession talks could begin on 3 October 2005. EU actors however appreciated the need to sustain Turkey's ongoing reform process over the course of the negotiations. Hence, the European Council foresaw a continuing EU role in determining Turkey's reform priorities through updated Accession Partnerships, in monitoring compliance through the Commission's progress reports and in threatening to suspend negotiations in the event of a stalling or backtracking of the reform process. In addition, the negotiating chapter on the 'judiciary and fundamental rights' impinged directly on political reforms. All seemed in place for an ongoing virtuous dynamic.

Yet over the course of 2005 and more acutely in 2006 and 2007, signals from both Ankara and Brussels indicated that the virtuous circle was dangerously slipping back into its vicious dynamics. In Turkey, the reform momentum slowed down, and there has been a new and worrying wave of prosecutions limiting the freedom of expression. A notable cause of this has been the establishment of the Great Union of Jurists by Kemal Kerinçsiz, which has made active use of the remaining illiberal aspects of Turkish law (e.g. Article 301 of the Turkish Penal Code) to prosecute activists and intellectuals, including the renowned cases

---

[2]Amendments made in 1997 to Sections 141, 142 and 163 and in 1999 to Sections 243, 245 and 354.

of Orhan Pamuk, Hrant Dink and Elif Şafak. On the EU side, Turkey-sceptic declarations by several European politicians, the French decision to hold a referendum on Turkey's EU entry and its criminalization of denial of the Armenian genocide, the EU constitutional crisis and its so-called 'Enlargement fatigue', the dispute over Turkey's recognition of the Republic of Cyprus and the French presidential campaign of May 2007 in which Turkish accession became an important issue, have all cast dark shadows over Turkey's EU future.

Reflecting Turkey-scepticism in the EU, Turkey's Negotiations Framework placed much emphasis on the open-ended nature of the talks, on the EU's absorption capacity and on the possibility of permanent derogations in key areas such as free movement of persons, structural funds and agriculture. Ultimately, the EU began accession negotiations in October 2005. But only a year after their official launch, negotiations—while avoiding a much-quoted 'train crash'—risked serious derailment. On the grounds of Turkey's non-implementation of the amended customs union protocol to include the Republic of Cyprus, the Union decided in December 2006 to suspend negotiations with Turkey on eight chapters of the *acquis*. While the suspension should not prevent Turkey from pursuing negotiations with the Union and aligning its laws and practice with the *acquis* (including on the suspended chapters). Yet in practice, this situation has re-instilled mistrust between the parties and could possibly result in a slowdown in negotiations. While not necessarily negatively prejudging Turkey's ultimate EU membership, this may dilute the domestic transformationist potential of the accession process.

Understanding the dynamics behind EU–Turkey ties

Particularly since EU–Turkey ties have been set in the framework of accession, EU decisions have profoundly affected the pace and form of Turkey's domestic developments. One primary cause of this interaction rests in the value accorded in Turkey to the goal of EU membership. Throughout its republican history, Turkey has consistently looked westwards in search of development models. Born from the ashes of the empire, the republic abolished the sultanate and the caliphate, severed its ties with its Ottoman past and overturned the religious-based nature of statecraft and social relations. Over the years, European secularism and nationalism, Westernization and modernization remained at the core of the Turkish state and nation-building processes. In the realm of foreign policy, Turkey sought recognition as a member of the Western family of nations. After the Second World War, the country joined the OECD, the Bretton Woods institutions, the Council of Europe, NATO and the OSCE. Moreover, Turkish authorities always manifested their interest in close ties with the European Community. Being part of the EEC was seen as the natural economic corollary of the country's geostrategic orientation. In the 1990s, as Turkey's European vocation translated into concrete membership aims, the EU dimension shifted in Turkey's domestic political realm.

Given the history of the Turkish republican project and its close association with Europe, the Turkish body politic initially reacted positively to the Copenhagen criteria. This was not least because the establishment genuinely believed that despite minor hiccups, Turkey already displayed the necessary prerequisites of membership. Ankara repeatedly claimed that Turkey had been a multi-party democracy since 1946, and that its strict adherence to secularism and faithful commitment to the West proved its democratic credentials. In addition, opinion polls regularly showed (up until 2005) that well over 70 per cent of the population backed the goal of accession. Membership was seen by the wider public as a means to enhance economic development, anchor Turkey to Europe, and thus accomplish Atatürk's long-standing aspiration of development through Westernization. In the light of a strongly favourable public opinion, no major political force could openly stand out against membership and its criteria.

Yet this primary explanation accounts neither for the ebbs and flows in EU–Turkey relations, nor for the uneven pace of Turkey's domestic transformation. To uncover the finer intricacies underlying these trends, it is necessary to delve into the ways in which EU decisions have affected domestic incentives and contributed to the relative empowerment of one set of domestic actors over another. Simply put, when EU decisions have been forthcoming, the credibility of conservative voices was tarnished, contributing to an acceleration of the reform momentum through the empowerment of reform-minded segments of the establishment. When EU trends turned away from Turkey, doubts and fears feeding Turkish nationalism and conservatism re-awakened, slowing down or reversing reforms.

This is because beyond the ostensible support for EU membership, closer scrutiny of the Turkish political scene reveals that positions towards the EU have been far more nuanced. Paying lip-service to the general Copenhagen criteria was one thing. It was quite another to have the determination to embark on the revolutionary reforms embedded in the accession process. In a country with extreme sensitivity on issues of national sovereignty, many of the EU's political requests were perceived as undue interference in domestic affairs. Many also felt the need to qualify Turkey's compliance with the criteria. The official discourse stressed the specificities of the Turkish case and particularly the security concerns which set it aside from other EU members and candidates. Other reform-minded actors instead supported membership precisely because of its entry criteria, which provided the necessary anchor to guide the country towards progressive change. Unlike conservative and nationalist actors, liberals and reformists viewed the Copenhagen criteria as welcome guidance rather than as the high price to pay for membership.

Hence, the profound yet differentiated impact of EU ties on Turkey. The leap from associate to accession candidate in 1999 provided the initial boost to reform-minded actors, by raising the value of EU contractual ties. But candidacy without negotiations made it abundantly clear that the process would not move forward without Turkey's political reforms. The target of opening negotiations, made more credible after 2002, thus explains the peak of reform activity in 2003–2004. In those years, reformers in Turkey appealed to the calls for change emanating from Brussels and to the encouraging signals given particularly in Copenhagen in 2002.

Yet on other occasions, EU decisions did just the opposite: unwittingly legitimizing conservative and nationalist forces, by awakening dormant Turkish fears about the EU's willingness to accept Turkey into its club. Mistrust of Europe is historically ingrained in Turkish society, deriving from memories of over two centuries of Ottoman retreat under European pressure and culminating in the trauma of the 1920 Treaty of Sèvres. Turkish nationalists/conservatives thus argued that Turkey should embark cautiously on EU-demanded reforms, given that Europe would not come to Turkey's rescue in the event of mounting instability. Moreover, they argued, the Copenhagen criteria could be used by the EU to tear the country apart. When mobilizing Turkish fear and mistrust, nationalists appealed to instances of EU exclusion and double standards. Even following the launch of the accession process, Turkish mistrust persisted. This was because, as Turkey made progress in reform, Turkey-sceptics in the Union could no longer easily hide behind domestic shortcomings when rejecting Turkey's membership. Other 'non-Copenhagen criteria' reasons started to be aired openly, summed up in the heightened concern about the EU's 'absorption capacity'. These included fears that Turkey's entry would dilute the loosely defined *'esprit communautaire'*, that it would result in rising Turkish immigration, lead to insurmountable institutional, economic, social and cultural (including religious) problems and pressures, and bring the Union dangerously close to the Middle East and Eurasia. The existence of such a debate raised Turkish mistrust and legitimized those who argued that EU-driven reforms should be kept in check, given the expectation that Europe would ultimately turn the cold shoulder to Turkey.

Endogenous determinants and their interaction with EU relations

The offer of membership on the one hand and the pending doubts concerning Turkey's future in Europe on the other provide a key explanation of the cyclical trends in EU–Turkey ties and the irregular pace of Turkey's domestic transformation. However, the latter has been determined principally by endogenous factors, as well as by international and regional developments. The key task is thus to assess how endogenous determinants have interacted with the wider EU dimension.

Party politics

The trends in Turkish party politics provide a first domestic determinant of the form and pace of reforms. The mid-1990s were characterized by a relatively high degree of instability in Turkish party politics. The 1995 parliamentary elections failed to produce a stable government and power oscillated between several unwieldy coalitions including the Islamist Welfare Party, which was ultimately ousted by the 'soft' military coup in February 1997. The exit of the Welfare Party in June 1997 failed to produce stability, resulting in the alternation of shaky minority coalitions until the 1999 elections. In terms of reform, this also meant that few steps were taken during those years and the EU was hardly forthcoming in its decisions regarding Turkey's EU membership. Most EU actors were inclined to see the 1996 customs union agreement as a substitute for rather than as a stepping stone to membership.

The 1999 elections saw the rise of a three-party coalition, led by veteran Bülent Ecevit (DSP) in alliance with the liberal Motherland Party (ANAP) and the nationalist National Action Party (MHP). Ecevit's government came to power on a reformist platform, focusing on the banking sector and the social security system, the reform of SSCs and the amendment of the law on political parties. Some legislative reforms were passed in 1999, providing an incentive to the European Council to accord candidacy to Turkey. However, following the formal launch of Turkey's accession process, the overall attitude of Ecevit's cabinet towards reform became increasingly cautious. This was primarily because of the dynamics within the coalition itself (the conservative impact of the nationalist MHP as well as the DSP, and the relative weakness of the liberal ANAP). Hence, in response to the priorities highlighted in the EU Accession Partnership in March 2001, Turkey adopted a National Programme, in which the government postponed the handling of the most complex political questions. The mounting tensions within the DSP–MHP–ANAP coalition came to a breaking point when EU pressure mounted in 2001–2002, making it abundantly clear that Turkey needed to show concrete reform progress in order to shift the accession process forwards. Hence, the EU-inspired reform programme moved to the centre of the domestic debate and the political forces repositioned themselves around the issue of EU accession. This was critical in triggering the August 2002 reform package and in leading the country to early elections in November 2002. Both the campaign and the elections were important litmus tests for the state of the debate on reforms and the EU, given that most political forces indicated that fulfilling the Copenhagen criteria was a top priority in their programmes.

The Justice and Development Party (AKP) obtained a landslide victory in November 2002, allowing for the formation of a single party government. Not only was the new government uncharacteristically strong and stable, it was also committed to an ambitious reform agenda. The AKP, which had been founded in 2001 after a split from the Islamist Felicity party, defined itself as a democratic-conservative party. While tapping into the socially conservative values of its core electorate, the AKP abandoned Islamism as a political programme. Its social conservatism coexisted alongside its commitment to modernization, secularism and democratisation, pegged on the EU accession anchor. The AKP government's commitment to political reforms and EU accession has important interest and ideology-related explanations. In terms of interests, commitment to reform and EU accession provided a much-needed legitimization of the party, allowing it to shake off domestic and international suspicions concerning its alleged Islamist agenda. Democratic reform and EU accession would also guarantee the AKP's political survival, given the unlikelihood of the party being banned like its predecessors under a liberal democratic system. In terms of ideology, reforms and accession allowed the AKP to articulate its calls for greater religious freedoms through a wider platform for individual rights and freedoms. The government proudly dubbed the Copenhagen criteria as the 'Ankara criteria'.[3] The rise of the AKP, together with the December 2002 decision to give a conditional date for the start of accession negotiations, provided the single most important explanation for the acceleration of the reform process in 2003–2004.

As discussed above, the reform momentum in Turkey has waned since 2005. Several interconnected reasons lie behind this. First and foremost has been the rise of nationalism in the country, which came to the fore with the public outrage at the burning of a Turkish flag during a March 2005 demonstration in Mersin and the widespread popular support for nationalistic novels and movies. Connected to this is the approaching deadline of the 2007 parliamentary elections and the AKP's desire to avoid losing ground vis-à-vis nationalistic campaigning by right- or left-wing parties, which in the aftermath of the presidential election debacle in April–May 2007 attempted to join forces in an effort to oust the AKP. Alongside rising nationalism, a second reason for the slowdown in reform is the

---

[3]Keynote speech by Minister of the Economy Ali Babacan at an informal EU–Turkey Brainstorming meeting organized by the EUI and Sabanci University, European University Institute, Florence, 6–7 May 2004.

fatigue effect following two marathon years of reform and the absence of adequate structures and incentives to ensure effective implementation. These domestic reasons have dovetailed with the EU's visibly waning commitment to Turkey's accession and its growing scepticism towards ongoing Enlargements.

The economy

A second domestic determinant of the reform process has been the state of the Turkish economy. Since its global opening in the 1980s and throughout the subsequent two decades, Turkey's economy took important steps forward in terms of growth and export capacity. However, the country's economic development had been hampered by deep macro-economic instability, giving rise to recurrent crises. The crises have had different impacts upon the country's political reform process.

Following a sharp economic contraction, mainly provoked by the Russian crisis and the 1999 earthquake, Turkey signed a new stand-by agreement with the IMF in December 1999. As a result of the IMF agreement, the DSP–MHP–ANAP government had to accept external (economic) conditionalities as part of domestic policy making, thus preparing the government to accept the intrusive EU political conditionality that came into effect after December 1999. Turkey made some progress in complying with the IMF loan conditions in 2000, reducing its fiscal deficit, tentatively proceeding with privatization and introducing a crawling pegged exchange rate to lower inflation.

Yet these initial successes were wiped away by two major economic crises which struck Turkey in November 2000 and February 2001. The initial spark of the crises was a political dispute between the prime minister and the president, which triggered a rush to the dollar in financial markets. The central bank attempted to defend the currency peg but lost over $7 billion and was almost immediately forced to float the lira, with an instant 36 per cent depreciation against the dollar. The crisis brought the economic reform programme to a halt and hit the real economy. Industrial production and GDP shrunk by 7.5 per cent by the end of 2001, while inflation rose to almost 70 per cent. Unemployment soared and Turkey entered its worst recession since the 1940s. However, the urgency of the crisis induced a wide debate on the country's structural illnesses, which quickly converged on the diagnosis and prognosis for the crisis. Half-hearted reforms were ruled out. Turkey could not afford to fall again into a cycle of short-lived adjustment, followed by uncontrolled public spending at the first signs of recovery. The political class had to lead the country towards long-term reform, increasing transparency and accountability, reducing the state presence, and eradicating corruption, cronyism and political influence over the economy. In March 2001, the government signed a $12 billion agreement with the IMF, subscribed to a new reform programme and appointed Kemal Derviş, a World Bank Vice-President, as Economy Minister. Banking reform, budget cuts and privatization were at the core of the reform programme. The political consensus over the paramount importance of economic reform also contributed to the renewed commitment to the political reform agenda promoted by the EU. The deep recession also generated high levels of public discontent with the government and a strong push for political change, which translated into the results of the 2002 elections. The financial crises were thus pivotal in projecting Turkey into a higher gear of its reform and EU accession process.

The accession process was aided further by the ensuing economic recovery and stabilization. With the exclusion of a brief interlude in the summer of 2002, the IMF programme remained on track and in late 2002 the economy started displaying sustained growth, with a quarterly average of over 7 per cent. Inflation was brought down to single digits, an historical achievement for the highly inflationary Turkish economy. In time, Turkey also succeeded in reducing fiscal imbalances, through fiscal discipline and an accompanying reduction in interest rates, which further reduced the cost of debt. The government also pursued important structural reforms, liberalizing electricity, sugar and tobacco prices, reducing agriculture subsidies, reforming the banking system and strengthening independent regulatory structures. Structural reforms boosted market confidence, further strengthening the government's hand in managing and financing public debt and external imbalances. A new agreement with the IMF, signed in May 2005, has continued to provide consistency and guidance.

Turkish steadiness and success in reforming the economy has been broadly recognized by international markets. Since 2001 EU exports to Turkey have being growing by almost 20 per cent per year, while its imports by around 13 per cent. Furthermore, Turkey is increasingly integrated in EU production cycles and has recently witnessed an important increase in foreign direct investments (FDIs) coming from the EU. However, the persistence of the virtuous cycle of growth and reform requires an ongoing positive perception of Turkey's progress at the international level. Much remains to be done to improve Turkey's capacity to cope with possible future shocks. Bureaucratic red tape, high tax burdens and corruption still hinder investment and growth. Unemployment remains above 10 per cent despite high growth rates. Turkey must continue to reform and modernize its economy in order to absorb a young and rapidly expanding workforce, entailing additional readjustment costs through a contraction of the agricultural and traditional sectors and an ensuing growth of the skilled manufacturing and service sectors. As such, the authorities must devote increasing attention to education, in order to improve the quality of the workforce and allow for the restructuring of the real economy.

The accession process should ease this process of economic reform and restructuring. However, this may run the risk of creating an EU backlash in Turkey, as the short-term losers from change may come to blame the EU for their ills.[4] It is indeed pertinent to note that since the opening of accession negotiations in 2005, support for the EU among Turkish public opinion has dropped dramatically from well over 70 per cent during the period from the late 1990s up to 2004, to just 44 per cent in the spring of 2006.[5] The inevitable transition costs embedded in the accession process heighten the need for EU actors to demonstrate their commitment to Turkey by supporting the creation of the 'soft infrastructure' necessary to hedge against the costs of economic change.[6]

---

[4]G. Sak, 'Turkey's transformation process and the risk of an anti-EU backlash', paper presented at 'The Bosphorus Conference', British Council/Centre for European Reform, Istanbul, 14–15 October 2005.

[5]Eurobarometer 65, European Commission, Spring 2006. Available at <http://ec.europa.eu/public_opinion/archives/eb/eb65/eb65_tr_exec.pdf> (accessed December 2006).

[6]K. Barysch, *The Economics of Turkish Accession*, Centre for European Reform, London, 2005.

The security dimension

The 'security dimension' has always been central in modern Turkish history, going well beyond the military sphere, and ranging across the political, social and economic domains. 'National security' in Turkey has had an all-encompassing definition, including the protection of the state's constitutional order, the national image, the state's integrity and interests, and its laws and principles.[7] In order to successfully address all the (real or perceived) threats to the country, the state, including the military, has used unsparingly and in a coordinated fashion all the policy instruments at its disposal.

The security narrative took root in the 1920s, in the wake of the Treaty of Sèvres and the subsequent Greek military occupation of Anatolia. Occupation gave rise to military resistance led by Mustafa Kemal, later known as Atatürk, whose victory led to the establishment of the republic. Unsurprisingly, the military came to affirm itself as the guardian of the normative foundations, the national security and the territorial integrity of the republic. The result of this was the periodical military coups in Turkish history, when the armed forces felt that politicians were compromising the basic tenets of the Republic. The coups turned the security narrative into a centrepiece of Turkish political life. The population became increasingly accustomed to hear military leaders speak on all major national issues and the army's status was reinforced by the public perception of the immaturity and corruption of the political class. After the military left power in 1983, an empowered National Security Council under the 1982 constitution became the institutional mechanism through which the military retained a say in policy making.[8] The military also had informal ways of influencing decision making. The Chief of Staff and other top officers made frequent interventions in public debate and their declarations were widely reported by the media. The most recent manifestation of this informal source of military influence has been the opposition to the presidential candidature of AKP number two Abdullah Gul, which has triggered a political crisis and early general elections in July 2007.

The security narrative has also been fed by other factors, and in particular by two real and perceived threats to the Kemalist republican order. Political Islam represented the first threat to the Turkish republican project, which was based precisely on the state's orchestrated secularization of society. Political Islam emerged as a threat to the secular Kemalist republic in the 1970s and 1980s, with the rise of Necmettin Erbakan's National Order Party (renamed National Salvation, Welfare, Virtue and Felicity due to the successive closures of the party). The political instability of the late 1970s and the electoral successes of Welfare in the 1990s represented the pinnacles of the Islamist threat in the form of a mass political movement. These peaks appear to be gone. But rather than the constitutional bans and repression on Islamist political parties, it has been the rise of the Justice and Development Party (AKP)—self-defined as a Muslim democrat democratic party—which has acted as the most powerful antidote against mass Islamist movements. The re-creation of a party with an Islamic background but

---

[7]A. Guney, 'The military politics and post cold war dilemmas in Turkey', in K. Koonings and D. Kruijt (eds), *Political Armies, the Military and Nation Building in the Age of Democracy*, Zed Books, New York, 2002, p. 166.

[8]On the Turkish military see G. Jenkins, *Context and Circumstance: The Turkish Military and Politics*, Adelphi Paper 337, IISS (International Institute for Security Studies), London, 2001.

with a forward-looking mandate to establish itself as a Muslim democratic party on the centre-right of the political spectrum has drained the life-line of radical political Islam. This is not to say that political Islam is a past phenomenon in Turkey. In view of the AKP's traditionalist platform and the strongly felt Christian discrimination against the Muslim world, religious identity in Turkey is on the rise. However, it no longer appears set to take the form of mass radical movements intent on reversing the country's secular order. It is indeed noteworthy that the AKP government itself, while having clear preferences regarding controversial political issues such as the headscarf ban or the status of religious vocational schools (*imam hatip* schools), has backed down from pressing for change in open confrontation with the secular establishment. The strong reduction in the perceived Islamist threat was the necessary domestic premise to undercut the security discourse in Turkey, thus allowing for political liberalization.

The beginning of the EU accession process came alongside these changes, providing the additional external impetus for the AKP to engage in reform. More precisely, the accession process provided the AKP with a politically acceptable framework within which to pursue political liberalization without raising too many eyebrows amongst the establishment. Alongside this, latching on to the accession process became the vehicle through which the AKP could shed its Islamist reputation within Turkey and the EU. This is not to say that the strong coincidence of interests between the AKP and the EU accession process is set in stone. On the contrary, the Turkish perception in 2006 of EU discrimination against Turkey on the Cyprus dossier or the European Court of Human Rights (Council of Europe) judgement that Turkey's headscarf ban does not constitute a violation of fundamental rights[9] has tarnished the appeal of 'Europe' amongst the AKP and its sympathizers.

Kurdish separatism, which in the 1980s and 1990s led to 35,000 deaths and multibillion dollar costs, has also fed the security discourse in Turkey. This interlocked with rising Euro-scepticism in Turkey in the context of the 1997–1999 nadir in EU–Turkey ties, particularly in 1999 when PKK leader Abdullah Öcalan toured Europe in search of a safe haven. The Öcalan affair reinforced the feeling that when territorial integrity and national security were at stake, Turkey could only rely on itself. Likewise, the re-eruption of violence in 2004–2005 coupled with the trends towards secession in Iraqi Kurdistan, have re-awakened dormant fears and nationalism in Turkey. More so than in the 1990s, rising Turkish insecurity and nationalism ignited by the Kurdish problem have acquired a distinctive anti-Western twist. Mounting tensions and mistrust between the EU and Turkey and the American invasion and occupation of Iraq have all conflated into a new anti-Western brand of Turkish nationalism.[10]

A final key variable influencing the security dimension in Turkey and its impact on the domestic reform and EU accession process is the changing role of the military itself. The political reforms undertaken under the accession process have downscaled the military's influence in politics. Institutionally, the NSC structure has been modified to introduce greater civilian control so as to respond to EU conditionality on civil–military relations. Clearly, without the military's

---

[9]Leyla Şahin v. Turkey, Application No. 44774/98, 10 November 2005.
[10]I. N. Grigoriadis, *Upsurge amidst Political Uncertainty: Nationalism in Post-2004 Turkey*, SWP (Stiftung Wissenschaft und Politik) Research Paper 2006/RP 11, October 2006.

tacit acceptance, these reforms would not have taken place. This acceptance is partly due to the military's general support for the accession process (particularly under former Chief of General Staff, Hilmi Özkök). It is also largely due to the fact that the armed forces have been slowly redefining their role within Turkish politics, appreciating that four military coups have not ensured long-term stability in the country.

However, when it comes to the complex terrain of security, changes are slow, irregular and reversible. Institutional changes do not automatically translate into a change in underlying norms, beliefs and policy practice. While sustaining and ascribing to the national security discourse, the military is likely to retain a key role in politics so long as the security narrative prevails. That narrative is still prevalent in the country and each and every reform must be carefully justified domestically, demonstrating how it would not threaten national security and republican values. Yet the security narrative is not set in stone. If, as and when the EU progressively includes Turkey in its own security community, Turkey's security narrative may well transform. By becoming an EU member, Turkey's problematic borders would become EU borders and the complex problems arising from its neighbourhood would be shared with the EU. The EU anchor would provide a guarantee from internal threats to secularism and ethnic strife, thus allowing for a full adoption of EU democratic standards, as well as the full incorporation of the Turkish armed forces in the emerging structures of European defence.

Conclusions

With the beginning of Turkey's accession process in 1999, EU–Turkey relations have entered a virtuous dynamic, which spilled into and catalysed progressive domestic reforms, unprecedented in depth and speed. Although incomplete, progress, particularly since 2001, has been widely recognized and celebrated. The EU has turned into one of the key external factors anchoring Turkey's reform. Developments in the EU provoke chain reactions in Turkey, which are difficult to control and anticipate. Hence, while moving in a positive direction, the hiccups in EU–Turkey ties hold the potential to disturb, if not to stall and reverse Turkey's reform process. Yet the EU alone does not and could not determine the form and pace of Turkish reforms. It is rather the interdependence and interaction between the EU and a set of internal factors that determine domestic transformation or the lack thereof.

One last and fundamental question is whether the momentum towards modernization and liberalization will persist irrespective of EU influence. In other words, to what extent are Turkey's reforms irreversible? Does Turkey still risk lapsing into the instability, violence and nationalism of the past, if the Union were to ultimately turn its back to Turkey? No conclusive answer can be provided yet. On the political front, the existing reform process has already shaken age-long beliefs and codes of action, changing threat perceptions and the adequate response to these. It has affected institutions structurally, it has empowered civil society and it has generated a wider societal appetite for democracy and rights, which is likely to persist in future. Yet the resurgence of old security threats (e.g. Kurdish separatism), new perceived threats (Turkey's feeling of exclusion from the 'Christian West' and its confrontation with the

'Muslim East') and a rise in extreme nationalism domestically (exemplified most dramatically with the assassination of Hrant Dink in January 2007), if coupled with the EU's rejection of Turkey, could well reverse the important steps forward made in the early 21st century. On the economic front, the claim to irreversibility is perhaps even more difficult to defend. Although the Turkish economy has shown signs of inherent strength, the country needs external anchors and the EU perspective to reap the fruits of the long pre-accession period in terms of FDI inflows, sustained growth and productivity. Overall irreversibility is thus far from assured. What is clear is that Turkey is still moving in a generally positive direction, which is nonetheless marred by moments of lull and possible steps backwards. Whether and when the inevitable negative shocks will remain isolated incidents on a generally positive path remains to be seen. What is equally clear is that at the current juncture, the EU dimension remains indispensable to ensure that the moment of irreversibility will be reached.

Conservative globalists versus defensive nationalists: political parties and paradoxes of Europeanisation in Turkey

ZIYA ÖNIŞ

The period since the December 1999 Helsinki summit has been a time of remarkable economic and political change in Turkey. The EU impact was already evident in the 1990s, with the 1995 Customs Union Agreement exerting a significant impact in terms of initiating important economic and political reforms. Yet arguably the real breakthrough occurred and the momentum of 'Europeanisation' gathered considerable pace, once the goal of full EU membership became a concrete possibility with the recognition in 1999 of Turkey's candidate status.[1] Political parties have emerged as agents of Europeanisation, while themselves being transformed in the Europeanisation process. The objective of the present paper is to highlight the role of political parties in Turkey's recent Europeanisation process and to underline some of the peculiarities of the Turkish party system and of some of the key parties as agents of economic and political transformation.

From a comparative perspective, the following aspects of Turkey's Europeanisation appear rather striking and paradoxical. Civil society actors have been much more active and vocal in their push for EU membership and the associated reform process than the major political parties. Within civil society, business actors and notably big business have emerged as central.[2] Turning to the parties, the 'Islamists' have been transformed much more than their 'secularist' counterparts. A political party with explicit Islamist roots, the Justice and Development Party (AKP), established itself as a vigorous supporter of EU-related reforms following its November 2002 election victory.[3] Yet another paradox is that many of the established parties on both the left and right of the political spectrum can be characterized as 'defensive nationalists', in the sense that they are broadly supportive of EU membership in principle but tend to be uncomfortable with key elements of EU conditionality. If membership could be accomplished without reforms, many of these parties would welcome the opportunity. Finally a central paradox is that 'social democracy' remains, for historical and other reasons, the element least affected by the ongoing

---

[1] On the recent Europeanisation and reform process in Turkey, see N. Tocci, 'Europeanisation in Turkey: trigger or anchor for reform?', and M. Müftüler-Baç, 'Turkey's political reforms and the impact of the European Union', both in *South European Society and Politics*, 10(1), April 2005.

[2] On the role of civil society in Turkey's Europeanisation process, see F. Keyman and A. İçduygu (eds), *Citizenship in a Global World: European Questions and Turkish Experiences*, Routledge, London, 2005.

[3] On the transformation of political Islam and the AKP phenomenon, see H. Yavuz (ed.), *The Emergence of a New Turkey: Islam, Democracy and the AK Parti*, University of Utah Press, Salt Lake City, 2006.

Europeanisation process. The fact there is no European-style social democratic party constitutes a serious weakness in the Turkish context, contributing to a process of lop-sided democratisation. The absence or weakness of social democracy is also critical in terms of the limitations it imposes on the nature and depth of the Europeanisation process. Political competition increasingly involves different segments of the 'centre-right', taking the form of a contest between 'conservative globalists' and 'defensive nationalists', with the former providing the main impetus for reform and the latter constituting a serious source of resistance.

The peculiarities of the left–right divide in Turkish politics: a European perspective

A European observer would be quite puzzled by the left–right cleavages in the Turkish party system. In European or Western democracies, party positions on socio-economic issues or policies constitute the main dividing line between parties located on the left and right. Centre-left or social democratic parties are traditionally distinguished by their concern with the status of the poor, their preoccupation with income redistribution in favour of weaker segments of society and their vision of a more interventionist state in economic and social affairs. Although social democratic parties have been undergoing a process of change in recent years in an attempt to adapt to globalization, their traditional concern with redistribution and active interventionism remain intact, albeit in a modified form. In addition to socio-economic policies, culture also constitutes a line of demarcation between right and left. In cultural terms, the European left is much more secular in outlook and its approach to the European Union is in terms of an open-ended political project. In this respect, it is not surprising that some of the major European social democratic parties, including the German SPD and New Labour in Britain, have become major supporters of Turkish accession to the EU, on the strict understanding that Turkey would be willing to apply the kind of democratic reforms needed to satisfy EU conditionality.

Turning to the Turkish context, a leading scholar argues that 'the "right" refers to a commitment to religious, conservative and nationalist values, while the "left" is defined primarily in terms of secularism' (Özbudun, 2006, p. 135).[4] Unlike their West European counterparts, political party positions on socio-economic issues do not neatly correspond to the standard left–right cleavage. Right-of-centre parties in general and parties of Islamist origin, in particular, have also displayed sensitivity towards issues relating to social justice and the position of the poor. Traditionally, such parties have utilized the notion of a paternalistic state, effectively combining this with nationalistic and religious discourse to appeal to broad segments of society. In turn, this enabled them to construct large cross-class coalitions which became a basis for significant electoral success. Indeed, a cursory look at the multi-party era clearly indicates the dominance of centre-right parties in the electoral contest. The Democratic Party of Menderes in the 1950s, the Justice Party era under Demirel in the 1960s, the ANAP years under Özal in the 1980s and the recent experience with the AKP

---

[4]E. Özbudun, 'Changes and continuities of the Turkish party system', *Representation*, 42(2), 2006, pp. 129–137. For a major study on the Turkish party system, see S. Sayari and Y. Esmer, *Political Parties and Elections in Turkey*, Lynne Rienner, Boulder, CO, 2002.

under Tayyip Erdoğan represent the continuity of the dominant centre-right tradition in Turkish politics. This has been effectively challenged only once, by the self-professed centre-left Republican People's Party (CHP) led by Ecevit during the mid-1970s.

Centre-right parties in Turkey have also effectively capitalized on what Şerif Mardin has described as the centre–periphery cleavage in Turkish politics.[5] According to Mardin, the main line of demarcation underlying the Turkish political system in the multi-party era has been a perennial conflict between a centralized, cohesive and heavily secularist state elite confronted by a culturally heterogeneous periphery with strong religious overtones. Centre-right parties have effectively utilized anti-state or anti-establishment sentiments to construct broad-based electoral support. In contrast, centre-left parties, with their strong organic links to the republican 'centre', failed to develop the kind of links with society at large needed to generate widespread political support. From a European perspective, the striking anomaly of the Turkish experience is that right-of-centre, conservative parties appear to be more 'society-centred', whereas left-of-centre parties appear to be more elitist and detached from society at large. This again renders the simple application of right and left rather problematic in the Turkish context. Indeed, looking at the most recent configuration of Turkish politics, with the AKP in government and the CHP as the main opposition party, one can locate traces of the 'centre–periphery paradigm', with the CHP as the party of the state and the secular elites *versus* the AKP as the party of the periphery or society at large.

In terms of commitment to Turkey's EU membership, the parties' ideological positions appear much more relevant in the European context. In the Turkish context, however, the parties' ideological orientation on a left to right axis has limited explanatory power. In Turkey, EU membership has been a goal of state policy in line with the broader objectives of Westernization and modernization and has been embraced by parties from both sides of the ideological spectrum. Mainstream political parties have on the whole been supportive of EU membership in principle. 'Hard Euro-scepticism', entailing the rejection of EU membership, is confined to fringe elements in the party system, namely, extreme leftists or nationalists and radical Islamists, who constitute a very small percentage of the total electorate.[6] Nevertheless, 'soft euroscepticism', involving a certain dislike of the conditions associated with full membership if not the idea of membership itself, is quite widespread and can be identified in political parties across the political spectrum.[7]

'Soft Euro-scepticism' surfaces whenever there is a reference to Cyprus, the Kurdish issue, the rights of Christian minorities and so on. It is fair to say that the

---

[5]For the classic article on the centre–periphery paradigm, see Ş. Mardin, 'Centre–periphery relations: a key to Turkish politics', *Daedalus*, Winter 1972, pp. 169–190.

[6]The 'red apple coalition' refers to an attempt to bring together nationalists on both sides of the political axis. Hard-core Euro-sceptics if one excludes the MHP and the CHP would be less than 10 per cent. However, if one includes the MHP and the CHP, whose Euro-scepticism is increasingly indistinguishable from hard Euro-scepticism, the electoral potential of this group would amount to at least 30 per cent.

[7]On Euro-scepticism in Turkey see H. Yilmaz, 'Swinging between Euro-supportiveness and Euroscepticism: Turkish public's general attitudes towards the European Union', in H. Yilmaz (ed.), *Placing Turkey on the Map of Europe*, Boğaziçi University Press, Istanbul, 2005, pp. 152–181.

CHP today, as the principal element of allegedly centre-left opposition, is dominated by the rhetoric of soft euroscepticism. This is quite a disconcerting phenomenon, since in practical terms the distinction between hard and soft euroscepticism becomes increasingly irrelevant in the sense that it becomes meaningless to talk about membership in the absence of reform. What is striking from a European perspective, however, is that there exist quite significant elements within the Turkish state, society and party system, which tend to think of membership and reform as independent and unrelated categories. This is clearly an important factor to take into account in terms of the sustainability of Turkey's Europeanisation drive and the ongoing reform process.

The peculiarities of the party system are important in the context of Turkey's Europeanisation drive for the following reasons. First, some of the key supporters of Turkish membership in Europe, namely, the social democrats, fail to find a direct counterpart in the Turkish context. In many cases, they have to work through indirect channels, such as civil society organizations, in order to be able to monitor and influence the reform process. Indeed, the CHP's membership of the Socialist International has been increasingly described as absurd, given the party's current positions. This lack of correspondence between social democrats in Europe and in Turkey clearly constitutes a handicap. Secondly, the AKP, which finds itself at the centre of the reform process and wishes to develop close, organic ties with like-minded political parties in Europe, finds itself in the awkward position of trying to forge links with Christian Democratic parties which are on the whole far less receptive to Turkish membership on cultural and economic grounds. Clearly, these factors create a fertile environment for the principal alternative to Turkey's membership, namely, the idea of a special status or 'privileged partnership'. One should not underestimate the potential for the growth of a broad-based coalition supporting a privileged partnership solution for Turkey, given that this perspective is deeply rooted in key segments of both the Turkish and European party systems.

The AKP as a key political actor in Turkey's recent Europeanisation process

Conceptual distinctions, such as the left–right divide and the centre–periphery, have some value in understanding the nature of Turkish politics. However, such distinctions can be confusing at the same time, given the difficulties of making sharp distinctions between 'right' and 'left', 'centre' and 'periphery', especially if one tries to employ these terms on the basis of their everyday usage in European politics. A differentiation along the lines of 'globalists' versus 'defensive nationalists' arguably provides a more precise and meaningful distinction in understanding recent realignments in Turkish politics, particularly in the post-Helsinki era.

The term 'globalists' refers to those segments of state and society which essentially have a positive view of globalization and see it as a phenomenon which provides opportunities for material improvement and the advancement of society in general. 'Globalists' tend to be 'integrationist' and 'reformist' at the same time. Those who hold a positive view of globalization also see European integration and Turkey's EU membership as parallel and positive processes. 'Europeanisation', in this context, becomes a mechanism, a framework or an intermediate route for a country like Turkey to cope effectively with and benefit from globalization. They also tend to be 'reformist', in the sense that they see economic and political reforms as a necessary condition in order to capitalize on the benefits of Europeanisation and globalization.

In contrast, groups whom we categorize as defensive or inward-oriented nationalists have, by and large, a negative view of globalization. Their politics is based on fear, in the sense that they see globalization as a process leading to the erosion of national sovereignty, in turn generating partition and an inability to preserve the existing borders. Their conception of globalization is a negative process whose risks and associated inequalities far outweigh its potential benefits. Defensive nationalists also perceive globalization and Europeanisation as parallel and complementary phenomena, but tend to view these processes in a rather negative fashion as working against the unity and the secular character of the Turkish state.

At the elite level, the 'globalists' camp would include secular liberals both within the state and society at large, moderate Islamists and Kurdish reformers. This bloc has become increasingly powerful in the post-Helsinki era, enjoying considerable public support on the basis of the expected material benefits of effective exposure to globalization and eventual EU membership. The defensive nationalist or anti-reform coalition, on the other hand, includes ultra-nationalists, hard-core Kemalists and radical Islamists as well as major labour unions. One can easily fall into the trap of putting all these groups into the same basket and exaggerating the degree of their anti-reformism or euroscepticism. For example, 'Kemalist hard-liners', who are extremely sensitive on issues like secularism and national sovereignty, at the same time favour Westernization. They find themselves in the awkward position of supporting Turkey's EU membership in principle, since opposition to the EU would signify an anti-Western stance inconsistent with the founding principles of the Turkish Republic. When it comes to reforms, however, they find themselves in a rather uncomfortable position. This is clearly the kind of dilemma that the Turkish military establishment faces at the moment. It would be misleading to argue that the military is firmly in the anti-EU camp. It would also be incorrect to suggest that the military has a negative view of economic globalization, given that as a powerful economic actor in its own right, it actively engages in and benefits from the globalization process. At the same time, there is no doubt that the military leadership is highly uncomfortable with many of the key political reforms sponsored by the EU and would like to maintain a privileged role for itself in Turkish politics. Hence, even a conceptualization along the lines of 'globalist/pro-reform coalition' versus 'defensive nationalist/anti-reform coalition' contains certain shortcomings. Such a distinction has considerable analytical value but, nevertheless, ought to be used with certain caution and reservations.

The 'globalist' versus 'nationalists' division cuts across party lines. Indeed, it is possible to find elements of both camps within the same political party. It would be interesting to consider in this context the coalition government of 1999–2002 which played an important role in initiating widespread political reforms in Turkey, including the abolition of the death penalty. The major government partner, the Democratic Left Party (DSP) led by Bülent Ecevit, would be considered much closer to the 'nationalist' bloc. At the same time, the party's MPs included influential figures such as the Minister of State for Economic

Affairs, Kemal Derviş, and the Foreign Secretary, İsmail Cem, whom one would clearly identify with the 'globalist' camp. The second major component of the coalition government, the Nationalist Action Party (MHP) would clearly be classified as a key element of the 'defensive nationalist' bloc, whereas the third and minor coalition partner, the Motherland Party (ANAP) led by Mesut Yilmaz, was firmly in the globalist/pro-reform coalition. In fact, Yilmaz's leadership was critical in pushing the coalition government to pass a large-scale reform package through Parliament in August 2002.

The AKP, which established its electoral dominance in 2002, clearly capitalizing on the negative impact of the major economic crisis of 2001 on the established political parties, currently constitutes the strongest and most vigorous element of the globalist/pro-reform coalition within the Turkish political party spectrum. In contrast to the divisions which existed within the DSP, for example, the AKP presented a broadly united front in its defence of the EU-related reforms and IMF disciplines. The case of the AKP again demonstrates that there is no neat correspondence between the left/right distinction and reformism versus anti-reformism. This is a conservative, right-of-centre party with explicit Islamist roots. At the same, however, the party leadership's commitment to reform has been much more pronounced than any of its predecessors or existing competitors. Between 2002 and 2004, in the presence of a double external anchor (IMF and the EU), the economy recovered swiftly from a major crisis. The democratisation reforms continued with an accelerating momentum. The AKP government also differed from its predecessors in terms of foreign policy initiatives. For example, for the first time in the recent era, a Turkish government was willing to contemplate an internationally acceptable solution to the Cyprus dispute along the lines of the proposed UN plan. The very pace of the reform process in Turkey resulted in the EU's historic decision of December 2004 to initiate accession negotiations, probably at a much earlier date than initially anticipated at the Helsinki Summit.

The challenge of defensive nationalism: has the AKP been losing its early reformist momentum?

The AKP further consolidated its electoral position in the municipal elections of March 2004. With the rising Anatolian bourgeoisie in its electoral coalition, the party leadership reaped the benefits of globalization and potential EU membership as a means of constructing and sustaining a broad-based electoral coalition. In opposition, the party had adopted a somewhat critical attitude towards the IMF. Once in office, however, the party leadership was sufficiently pragmatic and flexible to accept that full-scale recovery from a major economic crisis in a debt-ridden economy would not be possible without an IMF programme. Commitment to the latter and to EU membership were also important in terms of generating support on the part of big business and the foreign financial community who were initially rather apprehensive about the party, fearing that it could indulge in a new round of populist expansionism on the economic front while undermining the secular foundations of the Republic in the political sphere. Beyond the economic realm, a firm commitment to EU membership was important for the AKP in terms of displaying its pro-Western orientation and its broad commitment to secularism. In addition, the party saw the EU as a necessary safeguard to protect itself against the hard-core Kemalist or secularist establishment in domestic politics. The EU appeared to provide an additional space for moderate Islamists converted into Muslim Democrats to press for what they considered to be essential religious freedoms. Whilst the AKP leadership provided support for the democratisation agenda in general, the democratic freedoms they cherished most were related to religion. The most publicized issue concerned allowing female students to enter schools and universities wearing headscarves.

At the end of 2004, Turkey appeared to be on the right track. The EU made the critical decision to open accession negotiations. The economy was booming and the AKP government appeared to be fully in control, facing very little effective opposition from parties either on the left or the right of the political spectrum. By 2006–2007, a rather different picture started to emerge, with the AKP appearing to lose some of its enthusiasm and initial reformist zeal. The pendulum appears to have swung considerably in the direction of the nationalists and Euro-sceptics and public support for EU membership appears to have suffered a considerable decline. Fortunately, there is a line of continuity which deserves serious emphasis, in the sense that rapid economic growth has continued, with the government staying relentlessly within the fiscal limits imposed by the IMF programme. For a country whose performance in previous decades had been considered highly inadequate, the economy appeared to be doing extremely well in terms of attracting long-term foreign investment. Moreover, the economy appeared to be quite robust in withstanding various internal and external shocks during 2006.

In retrospect, several factors have contributed to rising nationalistic sentiments in Turkey, helping to swing the precarious balance in domestic politics away from the reformist elements towards the defensive nationalist/anti-reform coalition. Negative developments in Europe itself have exercised an unfavourable impact on Turkish politics, an observation which clearly highlights the crucial impact of signals originating in the EU on the perception and behaviour of key political actors in Turkey. The European project itself appeared to have reached an impasse, following the rejection of the proposed Constitutional Treaty in the French and Dutch referenda. The fact that Turkish membership emerged as a major issue of contestation in Austria during the 2004 European Parliament elections and in France, during both the 2005 referendum campaign and the May 2007 presidential elections, encouraged a popular belief in Turkey that EU membership was not a credible objective. A typical line of thought was that although accession negotiations had been formally opened, obstacles would be created to divert Turkish membership aspirations onto an inferior track of 'privileged partnership'. Indeed, this option has been openly advocated by the current German Chancellor, Angela Merkel and by the former French Interior Minister and new President, Nicholas Sarkozy. There is no doubt that the popular media in Turkey reflected and communicated these internal debates and developments in Europe in a rather unbalanced fashion. The existence of considerable sources of support for Turkish membership at the elite level in the EU was not sufficiently emphasized and the critical nature of the decision to start accession negotiations was pushed into the background. There was a tendency to portray the EU as a monolithic bloc, composed of countries and groups unanimously opposed to Turkish membership. Moreover, little interest was shown in the details of the European constitutional debate.

Yet another issue which helped to reverse the tide in the direction of defensive nationalists was Cyprus. The general mood in Turkey was that the AKP government had done enough to support a compromise solution to the Cyprus debate. The Turkish Cypriots appeared to provide unequivocal support for the re-unification of the island under the Annan Plan. After the 2004 referendum, it was up to the EU to reward them and put pressure on President Papadopoulos and the Republic of Cyprus to complete their side of the bargain. But with the Republic of Cyprus safely in as a full EU member from May 2004, the EU appeared from a Turkish perspective to be unable to act impartially and fulfil its initial promises. Moreover, the EU made it increasingly clear that the resolution of the Cyprus dispute was a pre-condition for Turkish membership and that talks would be blocked if Turkey failed to open up its ports and airports to Cypriot vessels. For the majority of Turkish people, even for some liberal intellectuals, this appeared to represent a dead end. The typical response was that ultimately a choice had to be made between eventual EU membership and giving up Cyprus altogether, in the sense that what would be imposed as a solution would be the current Greek Cypriot government's position of integrating the Turkish Cypriots as a minority group into their own society.

In addition to Cyprus, the resumption of PKK violence during the course of 2006 following a six-year ceasefire, helped to fuel nationalist sentiments even further. Again, the typical reaction was that EU circles were rather insensitive to terrorist activities in south-eastern Turkey, especially at a time when significant progress was being made in terms of extending far-reaching cultural rights to the Kurdish-speaking population. Soldiers have been dying in confrontation with the PKK and the tragic state of their families has been publicized in the media, causing widespread anger and resentment on the part of wide segments of society. Added to this, frequent references to the Armenian genocide in European circles, culminating with the French Parliament's decision to approve a bill criminalizing the denial of the Armenian genocide as a thought crime, have constituted yet another powerful impulse contributing to the growth of anti-European sentiments in Turkey.

Growing euroscepticism has gone hand in hand with the growth of anti-American or anti-Western feeling. The human costs of the American invasion of Iraq, the plight of the Palestinians, undue pressure on Iran at a time when Israel appeared to have a free hand in terms of invading Lebanon and Europe's paralysis to act, helped to generate an increasingly negative image of the West in a society where a majority of the population is deeply conservative and religious. Clearly all these developments placed the AKP government in a defensive position.

Perhaps the real turning point for the AKP came with the Leyla Şahin decision in November 2005, when the European Court of Human Rights (ECHR) rejected the appeal to allow the wearing of the headscarf. The significance of this decision from the AKP's viewpoint was that the space provided by the EU for promoting religious freedoms in Turkey appeared to be more restricted than was originally anticipated. Growing Islamophobia in Europe, mainly as a result of al-Qaeda and terrorist attacks, has contributed to a more restrictive position on issues of Muslim religious freedom. Hence, the possibility for the AKP to advance the demands of its core conservative constituency with EU backing increasingly appeared to be a rather unrealistic proposition. This left the party in an awkward position, in the sense that it made it increasingly difficult to reconcile the demands of its core constituency with the objective of maintaining a broad-based electoral coalition. There is a danger here of over-exaggerating the importance of this particular episode. We should take into account that the AKP has moved progressively to the centre of Turkish politics and is now considered by many analysts to be in line with the strong tradition of centre-right parties from Menderes' DP in the 1950s to Özal's ANAP in the 1980s. At the same time, one should not forget that the party has a strong Islamist connection, being a direct descendent of Erbakan's Welfare Party of the 1990s. Both the leadership and the rank and file of the party have a strong religious orientation. Hence, the signals sent by the EU are likely to exercise a disproportionate influence over the perceptions and actions of the AKP leadership and its core electoral support.

Finally, it is important to emphasize that rising Euro-scepticism is a phenomenon that tends to affect most countries engaged in the process of accession negotiations. The new Central and Eastern European members of the EU, for example, encountered such a phenomenon during accession processes. The tight social, technical and environmental regulations that have to be implemented during the accession period are costly and evoke resistance, especially on the part of small business units. A radical process of restructuring is also taking place in the agricultural sector, with a large number of workers losing their jobs and being forced to find new sources of employment. A certain element of the falling support for EU membership documented in recent opinion polls might be a reflection of these ongoing and costly processes of economic adjustment. At the same time, the Turkish situation is different from that of its Central and Eastern European counterparts, due to the fierce intra-EU debate around Turkish membership and its relationship to Europe's future self-definition, a debate which was virtually absent in the context of the previous Enlargement. This kind of debate, in turn, helps to create a domestic backlash in Turkey which renders the task of reformist elements far more difficult.

Why does the absence of a European-style social democratic party matter?

From the early months of 2005 onwards, there was plenty of evidence to suggest that the AKP government was progressively losing its initial self-confidence and pro-reform stance under the impact of a rather severe nationalist backlash. The new Anti-Terror Law, re-introducing a set of clauses designed to curb individual liberties, suggested a swing of the pendulum back to the old-style security state. Furthermore, the party was reluctant to abolish Article 301 of the Turkish Penal Code, which has been used as a mechanism for restricting free speech on the grounds of insulting the Turkish state and the Turkish nation. A number of prominent writers and journalists including Orhan Pamuk, Elif Şafak and Hrant Dink found themselves standing trial accused of attacking the Turkish state. There is no doubt that without strong pressure from European political circles and public opinion, they would have faced extended trials and possible imprisonment. The AKP's failure to repeal Article 301 raised considerable question marks about the party's real commitment to democratisation, beyond the narrow agenda of extending religious freedoms. On the Kurdish issue, the government's approach appeared to converge with the traditional repressive approach of the Turkish state. Admittedly, however, the violent tactics of the Kurdish nationalists rendered the task of any government committed to dealing with the problem through further democratisation particularly difficult.

It was also surprising that the EU accession process did not appear to be at the top of the policy agenda, despite the major decision to open accession negotiations in October 2005. The appointment of Ali Babacan, the Minister responsible for economic affairs, as chief negotiator signalled to both domestic and external circles that the accession process was not receiving sufficient attention. Given the complexity of the task involved, it would have appeared wiser to appoint an experienced figure above party politics to play a leadership role in the EU affairs. Similarly, the replacement of the Central Bank Governor became a heavily politicized issue. It would have been sensible to retain the former Governor, Süreyya Serdengeçti, a highly respected figure in financial and business circles. Increasingly, the party appeared to be promoting figures from its core electoral base to key government posts, providing substance to fears of creeping Islamization of Turkish society.

On the foreign policy front, some of the government's key moves, notably during 2006, appeared unbalanced, raising question marks concerning the party's Western or European orientation. The AKP government's foreign policy was overly proactive in some areas. A good example was the decision to develop bilateral relations with the Palestine Authority's new Hamas government without any attempt to secure the approval of the European powers. This was a strange move for the government of a candidate country already negotiating its accession. In contrast, there was no attempt to improve the rights of Christian minorities in Turkey, a point frequently emphasized in the European Commission's monitoring reports. A move in the direction of re-opening the Halki Seminary, a school for the training of Orthodox clergy, would have had tremendous symbolic significance in European circles and would have given the government a certain leverage and breathing space with respect to the Cyprus issue. It would also have provided substance to the frequent claim that Turkey could contribute to the development of a genuinely multi-cultural Europe. The outcome of these unbalanced moves was a decline in the uniformly high level of support given to the government in most European countries. The AKP's foreign policy moves increasingly projected the image of a party much more at home in the Middle East and the Islamic world, as opposed to a European-style party committed to secularism and a liberal vision of multi-culturalism.

The list of such observations can be extended. They tend to indicate the structural limitations faced by a conservative, religious-based party in carrying out the Europeanisation agenda. Electoral pressures, swings of public opinion and lukewarm signals from the EU are also relevant. However, these factors alone are not sufficient to provide a complete explanation of the deteriorating performance of the AKP government. What is also paradoxical is that the AKP has faced very little pressure from the left in the direction of extending and deepening the democratisation agenda. The new Anti-Terror Law and the trials of key novelists or journalists, clearly marking a major step backwards in the recent democratisation process, were only effectively opposed in the domestic sphere by liberal intellectuals, certain civil society organizations and fringe left-wing parties, such as the Freedom and the Solidarity Party (ÖDP). There was hardly any opposition from the established political parties at either end of the political spectrum. Indeed, without the pressure from key EU institutions such as the Commission and the European Parliament, domestic opposition would have made little impact in terms of blocking the path of such notorious trials.

This naturally brings us to one of the key paradoxes of party politics in Turkey, namely, the virtual absence of a European-style social democratic party with a mass following. Leader domination and the absence of effective intra-party democracy have been perennial weaknesses of Turkish political parties. Indeed, the major parties on the left in Turkey, namely, the DSP under Bülent Ecevit and the CHP under Deniz Baykal, can be considered as typical or even extreme examples of leader-dominated parties. Paradoxically, the apparently more conservative parties of Islamist origin have enjoyed a considerably higher degree of intra-party democracy than either of the principal left-of-centre parties.

In 2002, following a three-year absence, the CHP returned to Parliament as the official opposition. During the 2002–2007 parliamentary term, the party's opposition focused single-mindedly on a narrow understanding of secularism. Baykal projected the image of a leader who was prepared to court the military in order to oust an Islamist party from power. Effectively relegated to the background were many of the issues that could have formed the basis of a social democratic agenda, such as the reform of the state's economic role, the elimination of corruption, the decentralization of decision making and the provision of public services, the promotion of policies to encourage small and medium-sized businesses, and policies designed to combat gender inequality and women's subordinate position in Turkish society. Indeed, after 2002, the party's nationalistic reflexes came progressively to the fore, in such a way that the CHP has currently become virtually indistinguishable from Turkey's major ultra-nationalist party, the MHP. Ironically, in recent years the CHP has established itself as one of the strongest elements of the defensive nationalist bloc and is clearly trying to extend its electoral base by capitalizing on the rising nationalist and Euro-sceptic mood in the country. Unusually in a party which locates itself on the centre-left of the political spectrum, the CHP leadership does not display any enthusiasm for democratisation reforms. It is fair to say, for example, that the most vocal opposition to the proposed abolition of Article 301 originated from the CHP. Nor does the party seem likely to undergo a serious transformation in the foreseeable future. Baykal's grip over the party apparatus remains heavily intact and the electoral setback in the municipal elections of 2004 failed to create a serious internal backlash.

According to many observers of Turkish politics who approach the issues from a left-libertarian perspective and who identify with social democratic parties of the 'third way', a major opportunity was lost in the summer of 2002. A group of MPs who resigned from the DSP formed the 'New Turkey Party' (YTP) under the leadership of İsmail Cem. Also associated with the party was Kemal Derviş, the architect of the post-2001 economic recovery programme. Unfortunately, the party's fortunes faced a major blow when Derviş decided to join the CHP, anticipating that the new party would be unable to enter Parliament given the 10 per cent threshold level. This proved to be a tactical error, in the sense that Derviş and his colleagues with a globalist social democratic outlook were progressively marginalized within the CHP. The YTP itself was eventually dissolved. In retrospect, this was a lost opportunity in the sense that the YTP could have presented itself as a genuine progressive party on the left whose support could increase over time. A party of this type could have formed the basis of a proactive opposition to the AKP. Its role as an active source of opposition could have been critical, in terms of counteracting the observed decline in the performance of the governing party on the democratisation and EU fronts. For many secular liberals, the CHP is an increasingly unattractive option. However, such voters also find themselves in the awkward position of not being able to identify a genuine alternative to the AKP.

Conservative bias in the Turkish party system and the future trajectory of Europeanisation in Turkey

Historically, Turkey–EU relations have been a cyclical process. But the end of each cycle appears to have brought Turkey closer to the European core. The period from 1999–2004 can be interpreted as the upturn of the cycle, whereas the period since 2004 clearly corresponds to the downward phase, culminating with the events which precipitated the early elections of July 2007. A sense of historical perspective allows us to go beyond the current negative mood prevailing in both Turkey and the EU and entertain a certain degree of optimism concerning the future trajectory of Europeanisation in Turkey. Westernization and Europeanisation have become central pillars of state policy and are unlikely to be reversed. Moreover, having reached the point of accession negotiations, it is highly improbable that the political and business elites would throw away the prospect of full EU membership.

On the positive side, the AKP displayed considerable flexibility during its period in office in 2002–2007. For example, it tried at various times to introduce legislation aimed at satisfying the demands and aspirations of its core group of conservative supporters. The bill involving the prohibition of alcoholic beverages in public places was a striking example of this kind of strategy. Yet, when this faced with serious public criticism, the party postponed such measures for the future, rather than pressing ahead single-mindedly. One can identify several examples of this kind of pragmatic approach to political management, which can be interpreted as an asset on the part of the AKP.

The AKP's fortunes are also heavily dependent on the country's economic performance. In spite of some negative developments on the political front, Turkey's recent economic performance has been rather impressive. Inflation has fallen for the first time in three decades and during the past four to five years, the country has been recording the fastest rates of economic growth within the OECD. Although the distributional effect of this growth tends to be uneven, there is no doubt that large segments of Turkish society are benefiting from this process, at least in absolute terms. The EU anchor has played a critical role in this recovery, which seems to have the ingredients of a more durable process than any of the growth spurts of earlier decades which typically culminated in a major crisis. The economic benefits of a powerful EU anchor make it unlikely that a future AKP government would deviate from the Europeanisation option and move in a totally different direction. Despite recent setbacks such as the ECHR decision on the headscarf, the AKP has a better chance of accomplishing its underlying agenda on religious freedoms under the EU umbrella. The Europeanisation process of the past decade has been instrumental in transforming moderate Islamists into 'Muslim democrats' and softening (whilst clearly not eliminating) the underlying fault lines between the secular and religious elements of Turkish society.

Yet there are structural limits to the leadership role that an identity-based party such as the AKP can play in Turkey's Europeanisation process. Overemphasis on religion can become more of a liability than an asset over time, especially given rising anti-Islamic sentiment in Europe in the post-9/11 global environment. This makes it increasingly imperative to highlight the secular nature of Turkish society rather than its Islamic character. Turkey's strategic advantage in this context will not be Islam per se, but the ability to render Islam compatible with secularism and democracy. In this context, it will be extremely important for a new kind of left to emerge and take root at the very centre of the Turkish party system. This kind of social democratic party would have a completely different agenda from the present-day CHP. It would certainly be committed to secularism but to a liberal version of it, which is not openly inimical to the religious phenomenon and respects individual choice up to the point that it does not threaten the liberal democratic basis of the republic. A liberal interpretation of secularism would allow more space for certain kinds of religious freedoms whilst at the same time preventing a kind of creeping Islamization of Turkish society, a phenomenon which most liberals would be afraid of. Such a party would also have a deeper commitment to the Europeanisation project itself, rather than seeing the EU in a purely instrumental fashion as a transformative device for the Turkish economy and society. A political party or movement of this kind would also consider the specific ways in which Turkey could act together with other European states in contributing to the development of the European project. This kind of discussion and commitment to the goals of Europeanisation will become progressively more important as the accession process gathers momentum.

A social democratic party of this type would be much more internationalist or globalist in its outlook than the existing Turkish parties. An internationalist approach is perfectly compatible with a patriotic vision and love of one's country. In this context, one can think of state strategies which are likely to help Turkey benefit from the process of globalization. But the emphasis would not be on Turkey alone, but on Turkey as part of a broader European and international community. In that sense, this kind of vision would be quite incompatible with the kinds of defensive nationalism that we have outlined. A party of this kind would also exhibit the kind of vision necessary to make certain important compromises or radical moves which would have a tremendous impact in terms of accelerating Turkey's Europeanisation process. The party would be radical enough to consider such measures as the withdrawal of Turkish troops from Cyprus, the opening up of the Armenian border to free trade and other similarly radical moves which no political party in Turkey has been able to contemplate so far.

Finally, if further democratisation or democratic consolidation is an absolutely critical aspect of the Europeanisation process, the presence of a well-established centre-left party with strong internationalist and democratic credentials would play a crucial role. On issues like removing all the impediments to freedom of speech or combating gender inequality—the latter a critical deficiency of Turkish democracy—one should not expect the main impetus to come from the AKP or one of its other conservative variants. Thus, even if such a new social democratic party failed to obtain an electoral majority, it could still play a very important role as part of an active pressure group in close association with like-minded civil society organizations in Turkey. Furthermore, a political party of this kind would be an important channel for mobilizing and sustaining like-minded political actors in Europe who support Turkish membership.

Concluding observations

Turkey's recent Europeanisation process has been characterized by a number of paradoxical features. Civil society organizations, notably business associations, have played a more active role as members of the pro-EU/pro-reform coalition than the principal political parties. 'Islamists' appear to have been transformed more radically than their 'secularist' counterparts, with a conservative party of Islamist origin, the AKP, becoming the principal agent for Turkey's European transformation following the 2002 elections. Turkish politics in the post-Helsinki era can be better conceptualized as a contest between globalists and defensive nationalists, cutting across the left–right political spectrum.

Yet another paradox concerns the absence of a European-style social democratic party. This represents a major weakness both domestically, for democratisation reforms and externally, given that European social democrats constitute a major source of support for Turkish membership. The fact that the CHP, the principal opposition party in 2002–2007, is as conservative and nationalistic as some of its centre-right counterparts, clearly suggests that simple applications of the concepts of left and right contain limited analytical value in terms of identifying the degree of reform orientation of individual parties. A central observation is that party politics in Turkey has a certain conservative bias, with competition taking place primarily among different centre-right parties. Clearly, this kind of one-legged or one-dimensional party system constitutes an important handicap from the point of democratic consolidation.

The paper has also tried to explain the recent reversal in the fortunes of the Europeanisation process in Turkey following the golden era of 1999–2004, due to a severe nationalist backlash which left the AKP government in a rather subdued and defensive position, especially in relation to the democratisation component of the reform process. In the medium term, our guess is that a newly elected AKP government would be likely to re-activate and accelerate the Europeanisation process. At the same, there exist structural limits to AKP's reformism, especially on the democratisation and foreign policy fronts. There is clearly a need for a new kind of social democratic party which would be globalist in orientation and have a deeper commitment to Europeanisation and reform than any of the existing parties. Whether such a party will actually emerge is hard to predict at this point, although one could safely predict that the CHP will not transform itself in this particular direction.

Europeanisation through EU conditionality: understanding the new era in Turkish foreign policy[1]

MUSTAFA AYDIN and SINEM A. ACIKMESE

Since October 2001, Turkey has embarked upon a process of wide-ranging political reforms through harmonization packages to redress its shortcomings vis-à-vis the Copenhagen criteria. The Turkish economy has already undergone substantive changes to become a fully functioning market economy and acquire the capacity to cope with competitive pressures. Alongside political and economic changes, Turkish foreign policy (TFP) is also experiencing a transformation as a result of European conditionality.

Since the EU's acceptance of the Turkish candidacy in 1999, TFP has been profoundly altered. For instance, without the prospects of EU accession, it would have been difficult to imagine Turkey opening the doors to internal debate on the 'Armenian issue' or the shift in the dialogue on Cyprus from a confrontational line to a 'win–win' discourse. Similarly, there was a distinct contrast between Turkey's attitudes towards Syria in 1998 and Greece in 1999 in response to their support for Abdullah Öcalan. While Syria faced troop mobilization on its border and threats of war should it not expel the leader of the separatist Kurdish group PKK from Damascus, the latter only received a diplomatic reprimand—and not a very strong or sustained one—when it was revealed that Öcalan had been sheltered in the Greek Embassy in Nairobi. What followed in both cases was a 'spring' in relations, the former achieved by coercive methods and the latter by a gentle push towards embarrassment.

This paper examines TFP in the framework of Europeanisation, to find out to what extent this approach is helpful in understanding change in the course of the last decade. First, it offers a brief discussion of the concept of Europeanisation as understood in European integration studies, focusing on its domestic dimension. Second, it analyzes modes of change in the foreign policy domain of EU member and candidate countries, showing that foreign policy Europeanisation of would-be members takes place through the conditionality provided in the CFSP (Common Foreign and Security Policy) *acquis*. Third, it introduces mechanisms of EU conditionality for foreign policy change in Turkey with specific references to institutional issues, traditionally sensitive foreign policy problems and the neighbouring region of the Middle East. The paper argues that while Europeanisation is the major framework for understanding the recent changes

[1]Research for this paper was funded by the State Planning Organization of Turkey through a project titled 'Comparative Analysis of Turkey and EU's Foreign and Security Policies in the New Neighbourhood'.

in TFP, domestic and international factors should also be taken into account to have a coherent overall picture.

Europeanisation: a new framework for analyzing the EU dynamics?

Europeanisation has been used in diverse ways in different social science disciplines.[2] From the *political science* perspective, it refers to the process of change at the domestic level due to the pressures generated at the EU level. From an *anthropological* perspective, it is widely depicted as a 'strategy of self-representation and a form of identification of people'.[3] Meanwhile, from the perspective of economists, the formation of 'various modes of inter-state cooperation, up to and including regional integration' in Europe is understood as Europeanisation.[4] Since the 1990s, the concept of Europeanisation has attracted renewed attention from *political scientists* specializing in European integration at a time when the EU was preoccupied with deepening. For these scholars, Europeanisation appeared as a new research agenda for understanding the dynamics of European integration both at the supranational and domestic levels. Since then, three different conceptualizations of the term have emerged within the boundaries of political science.

Following the traditional understanding of European integration through the prisms of neo-functionalist and/or intergovernmental theories, the first conceptualization concentrates on the creation of a European centre. In this 'bottom-up' approach, Europeanisation is the 'evolution of European institutions as a set of new norms, rules and practices', which formalize and regularize interactions among the actors.[5] The mirror-image of this conceptualization with its 'top-down' connotation, reflects Europeanisation as a process of domestic change that can be attributed to European integration. The most cited definition in this 'Europeanisation-from-above' suggests that it is a 'process reorienting the direction and shape of politics to a degree that EC political and economic dynamics become part of the organisational logic of national politics and policy-making'.[6] Apart from politics, policies and polity, the domain of change at the domestic level is generally seen in a wider spectrum covering styles, informal

---

[2]For a detailed historical perspective on Europeanisation, see M. Geyer, 'Historical fictions of autonomy and the Europeanisation of national history', *Central European History*, 22, September–December 1989, pp. 316–342 and L. Mjøset, 'The historical meanings of Europeanisation', *Arena Working Papers*, 24, University of Oslo, Oslo, 1997.

[3]J. Borneman and N. Fowler, 'Europeanisation', *Annual Review of Anthropology*, 26, 1997, p. 493. Also from the anthropological perspective, see V. Gransow, 'The end of ideological age: the Europeanisation of Europe', *Argument*, 24, March 1982, pp. 299–300 and H. Olafsdottir *et al.*, 'The Europeanisation of drinking habits in Iceland after the legalization of beer', *European Addiction Research*, 3, 1997, pp. 59–66.

[4]J. J. Andersen, 'Europeanisation in context: concept and theory', in K. Dyson and K. H. Goetz (eds), *Germany, Europe and the Politics of Constraint*, Oxford University Press, Oxford, 2003, p. 41. Also from the economic perspective, see G. Escribano and A. Lorca, 'The ups and downs of Europeanisation in external relations: insights from the Spanish experience', *Perceptions*, 9, Winter 2004–2005, pp. 131–158.

[5]T. A. Börzel, 'Pace-setting, foot-dragging and fence-sitting: member state responses to Europeanisation', *Journal of Common Market Studies*, 40, June 2002, p. 193; and Harmsen and Wilson, op. cit., p. 14.

[6]R. Ladrech, 'The Europeanisation of domestic politics and institutions: the case of France', *Journal of Common Market Studies*, 32, March 1994, p. 69.

rules, ways of doing things, shared beliefs and norms.[7] The third conceptualization in the literature is a merger of the top-down and bottom-up approaches that portrays Europeanisation as 'an ongoing, interactive and mutually constitutive process of change linking national and European levels, where the responses of the Member States to the integration process feed back into EU institutions and policy processes and vice versa'.[8] This approach considers Europeanisation as a cycle of interactions and change at all levels, and does not attach any analytical primacy either to centre-building or to domestic change, instead seeing them as coexisting in a vicious circle.

However, this cycle should be stopped at some point in order to achieve a methodological consistency, since 'being bound up in a circular movement is of little help as it blurs the boundaries between cause and effect, dependent and independent variable'.[9] Selecting one dimension of this process, either top-down or bottom-up, will bring more methodological clarity. As the aim of this paper is to understand the transformation of TFP within the conceptual framework of Europeanisation, the term will be applied in its top-down version, implying change at the domestic level triggered by the dynamics of European integration. The domestic level here should not be understood only within the context of EU member states, but should be conceptualized as 'covering the consequences of fulfilment of EU requirements and of voluntary orientation towards EU standards in candidates'.[10]

Europeanisation of national foreign policies: socialization or conditionality?

Compared to the literature analyzing the impacts of various EU policies under the EU's first pillar, *Europeanisation of national foreign policies* of either EU insiders or would-be members is a relatively overlooked topic. In one of the limited number of studies to date, Tonra explains Europeanisation in foreign policy as a

> transformation in the way in which national foreign policies are constructed, in the way in which professional roles are defined and pursued and in the consequent internalisation of norms and expectations arising from a complex system of collective European policy making.[11]

It was rare before the 1990s to find references in the literature to such a process of bringing about a common understanding on foreign policy at the European Community level, since the then EC lacked relevant competencies apart from the

---

[7]C. M. Radaelli, 'Whither Europeanisation? Concept stretching and substantive change', *European Integration Online Papers*, 4, 2000, p. 3; also available at http://eiop.or.at/eiop/texte/2000-008a.htm

[8]C. Major, 'Europeanisation and foreign and security policy: undermining or rescuing the nation state?', *Politics*, 25, September 2005, p. 177. For further analyses of synthesized perspectives, see Börzel, op. cit., pp. 193–214; K. Featherstone, 'Introduction: in the name of Europe', in K. Featherstone and C. Radaelli (eds), *The Politics of Europeanisation*, Oxford University Press, Oxford, 2003, p. 6; C. M. Radaelli, op. cit.

[9]C. Major, op. cit., p. 177.

[10]Ibid., p. 178.

[11]B. Tonra, 'Denmark and Ireland', in I. Manners and R. G. Whitman (eds), *The Foreign Policies of European Union Member States*, Manchester University Press, Manchester, 2000, p. 245.

modest experience of European Political Cooperation.[12] With the CFSP since the early 1990s, however, pursuing a more comprehensive security approach, adaptation of national foreign policies has been explored more extensively by European integration scholars.

The capacity of CFSP to reorient national foreign policy structures of member states is a 'surprise' for Smith, since 'there is a usual great sensitivity among most governments about foreign policy as a special domain in which national concerns dominate international or European interests'.[13] Apart from the issues of *domaine réserve*, he argues that CFSP, squeezed in the intergovernmental second pillar, does not have the competence to impose change on member states' foreign policies, when compared to the 'EU's capacity to impose extensive, explicit demands on its members in the form of treaty articles, secondary legislation, court cases and so within the socio-economic areas of the integration project'.[14] The mechanism of Europeanisation in the first pillar is 'formal penetration'[15] through 'obligatory implementation of EU law',[16] which can be characterized as vertical, hierarchical and non-voluntary. However, in the second and third pillars, such an hierarchical mechanism is out of question and decision making is mainly based on intergovernmental thinking. Thus, the EU lacks an authoritative, supranational, centralized actor in CFSP to impose change on national foreign polices of member states.

Since the EU cannot create sufficient pressure for change, there must be a reason why member states voluntarily transform their foreign policies in the direction of CFSP. In this respect, as the member states take foreign policy decisions mainly by consensus,[17] the following step would logically be domestic adaptation to the relevant CFSP tools in the form of a common strategy, common position or joint action.[18] To put it more precisely, the decision which member states take at the EU level through consensus is the same decision they have to adopt at the domestic level. However, transformation in member states' foreign policies due to EU dynamics should not just be reduced to the level of individual foreign policy actions. At the macro-level, through the mechanism of elite socialization[19] within the CFSP structures, member states have 'moved the conduct of national foreign policy away from the old nation-state national sovereignty model towards a collective endeavour'.[20] This does not mean that member states always act in uniformity

---

[12]For early accounts of Europeanisation in this domain see references of Featherstone, op. cit., p. 10.

[13]M. E. Smith, 'Conforming to Europe: the domestic impact of EU foreign policy cooperation', *Journal of European Public Policy*, 7, 2000, p. 614.

[14]Ibid., p. 613.

[15]P. Mair, 'The Europeanisation dimension', *Journal of European Public Policy*, 11, April 2004, p. 341.

[16]C. Major, op. cit., p. 180.

[17]Although the use of qualified majority was extended to a certain limit by Article 23 of the Treaty of Amsterdam, unanimity still remains the general principle of the decision making under the CFSP pillar.

[18]The only exception to this logic would be the rule of constructive abstention introduced by Article 23 of the Treaty of Amsterdam. In this context, member states that abstain from a decision taken unanimously by the other members, may not need to implement the decision in their foreign policies.

[19]Through the CFSP communication channels, national foreign policy elites are socialized to the extent that there appears a club-like atmosphere which is conducive to the forging of a common position on a number of difficult foreign policy issues. This is what Smith defines as the process of 'elite socialisation'. See, M. E. Smith, op. cit., pp. 618–619.

[20]C. Hill and W. Wallace, 'Introduction: actors and actions', in C. Hill (ed.), *The Actors in Europe's Foreign Policy*, Routledge, London, 1996, p. 6.

on every foreign policy issue. Nevertheless, through their transnational interactions they have learned the value of acting together.

However, this version of Europeanisation, applicable to the foreign policy transformation of member states, cannot offer a mechanism for analyzing the alteration in the foreign policies of would-be members. In the case of potential EU entrants, Europeanisation in every area takes place through EU conditionality.[21] As a concept initially developed for Central and Eastern European Countries, conditionality has become a general framework for understanding the internal shifts in candidate countries towards convergence with the EU. In the last round of enlargement in 2004–2007, conditionality was formalized through the Copenhagen/Madrid criteria of 1993–1995 and stipulated in Accession Partnerships, Regular Reports and Strategy Papers and Negotiating Frameworks. Under the EU's formal criteria, states wishing to enter the Union have to show stable institutions guaranteeing democracy, the rule of law, human rights and respect for protection of minorities; a functioning market economy and the capacity to cope with competition and market forces in the EU; and the capacity to take on the obligations of membership, including adherence to the objectives of political, economic and monetary union and the adoption of the *acquis* and its effective implementation through appropriate administrative and judicial structures.

In the foreign policy domain, the conditionality burden for the new entrants essentially came under the latter criterion of adopting and implementing the CFSP *acquis* which 'is essentially based either on legally binding international agreements or on political agreements to conduct political dialogue in the framework of CFSP, to align with EU statements, and to apply sanctions and restrictive measures where required'.[22] Before their accession, the recent entrants participated in the political dialogue and aligned themselves gradually with EU positions and actions. Failure to do so would have hindered their membership.

In contrast to the foreign policy changes of member states brought about by EU dynamics, the transformation of candidates is imposed vertically by the EU through an hierarchical process. Despite this substantial difference, the mechanisms influencing the foreign policies of current and would-be members have two common aspects. First, like the process of change for member states, Europeanisation of the candidates' foreign policies through conditionality is a voluntary process in the sense that it is the will of the candidates to join the EU; therefore they obey the rules of the club voluntarily. Second, regardless of whether change takes place within either a candidate or a member state, it is hard to differentiate the EU impact on this transformation from domestic and international factors. Foreign policy change might result from endogenous inputs (e.g. national reform projects, party politics, political events, public pressure or pressure groups) or exogenous influences (e.g. global politics, other institutions or regimes, developments in the target area or systemic changes) at a time when the dynamics of Europeanisation are also to the fore.[23] Therefore, even though at first glance, CFSP could be regarded

---

[21]On conditionality, see H. Grabbe, 'European Union conditionality and the Acquis Communautaire', *International Political Science Review*, 23, 2001, pp. 249–268.

[22]This phrase appeared in the final Comprehensive Monitoring Reports on Preparations for Membership of the 2004 entrants in November 2003.

[23]For domestic and international factors, see Jordi Vaquer i Fanés, 'Europeanisation and foreign policy', *Observatori de Política Exterior Europea Working Paper*, 21 April 2001, available at http://selene.uab.es/_cs_iuee/catala/obs/m_working.html.

as the independent variable for change, either through conditionality or socialization, endogenous and exogenous intervening variables should also be taken into account when studying national foreign policy transformation.

Europeanisation of Turkish foreign policy?

To understand the twists in TFP through Europeanisation, the conditionality concept should be analyzed as the mechanism that fosters change. In the Turkish case, the EU currently employs three types of foreign policy conditionality. First, as in previous enlargements, is *conditionality through the CFSP acquis*, through which Turkey is required to adopt and implement the *acquis* including '... joint actions, common positions, declarations, conclusions and other acts within the framework of the common foreign and security policy'. Second is *conditionality through political criteria*, which stands at the top of the membership conditions for any country wishing to join the EU. In contrast with the other criteria, negotiations with a candidate cannot begin until that country is regarded as having sufficiently fulfilled the political criteria. If a condition is stipulated as part of the political criteria, non-compliance during the negotiations may lead to suspension of talks, delaying membership. Third, the EU prescribes change in TFP through its determination on peaceful settlement of disputes between would-be members and their neighbours. The fourth paragraph of the Helsinki Presidency Conclusions in 1999 asserted that the candidates 'must share the values and objectives of the EU as set out in the Treaties', stressing 'the principle of peaceful settlement of disputes' and urging candidates 'to make every effort to resolve any outstanding border disputes and other related issues'.[24]

By embracing the principle of peaceful dispute settlement as one of its founding values, the EU has constructed it into another requirement for accession. This type of conditionality deriving from EU values had already been applied in the context of previous enlargements, although at that time it was evaluated under the CFSP chapter. The EU appeared less concerned with this 'criterion' previously, presumably because only a few of the candidates (Cyprus and to a lesser extent, Slovenia and Romania), had major problems with a neighbouring country. In the case of Cyprus, due to pressures originating from Greece, the member states circumvented the conditionality clause.[25] However, for Turkey and all current candidates, this criterion has been elevated onto an equal footing with the political criteria. Even though the EU does not officially and formally state that the resolution of disputes within the candidates' neighbourhood is a political criterion, the evaluation of these countries' advance in this domain under the political criteria chapter in every progress report reveals

---

[24]For the Helsinki Presidency Conclusions of 10–11 December 1999, see http://europa.eu.int/council/off/ conclu/dec99/dec99_en.htm.

[25]After Greece positioned itself to block the whole Enlargement process if Cyprus was not included, paragraph 9(b) of Helsinki Presidency Conclusions acknowledged that 'the European Council underlines that a political settlement will facilitate the accession of Cyprus to the European Union. If no settlement has been reached by the completion of accession negotiations, the Council's decision on accession will be made without the above being a precondition.'

that in effect, the EU considers it to be such.[26] Accordingly, this type of conditionality deriving from EU values and incrementally introduced into progress reports could be labelled as *conditionality through de facto political criteria*. We will now move on to examine how these three forms of conditionality have been applied in the Turkish case.

Conditionality through political criteria: civilianization of Turkish foreign policy

Traditionally, the military authorities have played a decisive role in the conduct of Turkish foreign and security policy. However, since 1999, the EU has pressed Turkey to align civilian control of the military with the practice in EU member states, mainly through reforms in the composition and policy-shaping role of the National Security Council (NSC). Originally established by the 1961 Constitution as an advisory body with a civilian majority to serve 'as a platform for the military to voice its opinion on matters of national security', the NSC has transformed itself over time into a powerful institution led by the military, whose 'recommendations would be given priority consideration by the council of ministers'.[27] Through these recommendations, which define the threats facing the country and provide for integrated domestic, foreign and military policies relating to national security, the NSC has become one of the most prominent actors in Turkish foreign policy making since the early 1980s. With its ability to supervise the implementation of these recommendations, the role of the NSC expanded further. Since its military members always spoke with one voice, they were able to create a security-conscious foreign policy with strong military contours.

On the path to Turkey's accession, the prevailing demand of the EU was to change the composition of the NSC, incorporating more civilians and a civilian Secretary General; as well as aligning its role as an advisory body to the Government in accordance with the practice of EU member states.[28] Accordingly, the Turkish Parliament passed a reform package on 23 July 2003, changing the structure and working procedures of the NSC. The government also appointed a new civilian Secretary General of the Council in August 2004, amended the laws to introduce a majority of civilian members of the Council, and introduced new rules of conduct for accountability and transparency.[29] Above all, the NSC Secretariat no longer has the authority on behalf of the President and Prime Minister to monitor the implementation of the NSC's recommendations. Thus, EU pressure has been instrumental in changing the balance within the NSC in favour of civilians, paving the way for a civilianized foreign policy.

---

[26]For instance, regional issues and international obligations are dealt with under the heading of political criteria in the 2005 and 2006 Progress Reports of Croatia and Macedonia, in both of which it is stated that 'regional cooperation and good neighbourly relations form an essential part of the process of moving towards the European Union'.

[27]Umit Cizre Sakallioglu, 'The anatomy of the Turkish military's political autonomy', *Comparative Politics*, 29, 1997, p. 157.

[28]See Accession Partnership 2001, paragraph 4.2 on enhanced political dialogue and political criteria.

[29]On the NSC reforms, see M. Heper, 'The Justice and Development Party government and military in Turkey', *Turkish Studies*, 6, 2005, p. 220.

In a country with an enduring tradition of military involvement in politics, it is highly unlikely that these reforms would have taken place if EU entry had not been at stake. Thus, the shift in the institutional dimension of TFP can be explained within the framework of Europeanisation through conditionality. However, EU conditionality has not yet been successful in preventing senior military officials from expressing their opinions on foreign policy issues, including relations with neighbouring countries.[30]

Conditionality through de facto political criteria: policies towards Greece and Cyprus

Turkish–Greek relations have improved dramatically since 1999 and Turkish policy towards Cyprus has changed substantially. It is doubtful 'whether there would have been the same kind of improvement in Greek–Turkish relations and a turnaround in Turkey's Cyprus policy without the EU'.[31] It is hereby argued that this major transformation has been due to vigorously applied conditionality, non-adherence to which would have blocked negotiations.

In Greek–Turkish relations, the historic rivals that had come to the brink of war on numerous occasions have since 1999 embarked on a seemingly sustainable period of easing up.[32] The change is evident in the increased level of official visits between the two countries, ongoing 'exploratory talks' between foreign ministries, the building of direct links between the armed forces of the two countries, the removal of landmines along the border, the reduction of military exercises and the exchange of information about them, as well as the inauguration of a natural gas pipeline project in July 2005. The positive trend at the official level has been accompanied by positive statistics in inter-societal and trade relations,[33] indicating a deepening of the relationship, despite the unresolved underlying disputes regarding the territorial waters, airspace and continental shelf in the Aegean.

This fundamental change has been explained by some analysts with reference to the close personal relations between the two foreign ministers in 1999, İsmail Cem and George Papandreou, who both favoured constructive dialogue. For others, it was the earthquakes of the same year which brought the two countries together.[34] Besides such simplistic analyses, it is clear that the turnaround has been related to Turkey's EU integration and to the growing rapprochement

---

[30]As far as the EU is concerned, 'statements by the military' should only concern military, defence and security matters; should be made under the authority of the government; and should avoid comments regarding relations with neighbouring countries without proper civilian supervision. See Commission of the European Communities, *Turkey 2006 Progress Report*, 8 November 2006, pp. 7–8.

[31]K. Kirişçi, 'Turkey's foreign policy in turbulent times', *Chaillot Paper*, 92, EU–ISS, Paris, September 2006, p. 58.

[32]On the evolution of Greek–Turkish relations before and after 1999, see M. Aydın and K. Ifantis (eds), *Greek–Turkish Relations; Overcoming the Security Dilemma in the Aegean*, Routledge, London, 2004; and A. Heraclides, 'Greek–Turkish relations from discord to détente: a preliminary evaluation', *The Review of International Affairs*, 1, 2002, pp. 17–32.

[33]The number of Greek nationals visiting Turkey increased from just under 150,000 in 1996 to more than half a million in 2005. Trade boomed from US$300 million in 1999 to over US$1.8 billion in 2004. See Kirişçi, op. cit., p. 21.

[34]For these views see Aydın and Ifantis, op. cit.

of Greek and Turkish civil societies, encouraged by EU funding.[35] Although rapprochement between the two sides appeared inconceivable after the capture of PKK leader Öcalan while leaving the Greek Embassy in Kenya, the dynamics of conditionality and the pull of integration contributed to a transformation of Turkey's response towards a more subtle reaction. Without the dynamics of conditionality, Turkey (and Greece) would not have embarked upon such an unprecedented journey. The map for this change has been provided by the EU in various documents such as the Accession Partnerships, Regular Reports and the Negotiating Framework. For example, the 2001 and 2003 Accession Partnership Documents called on Turkey, in the context of the political dialogue, to 'make every effort to resolve any outstanding border disputes and related issues, as referred to in point 4 of the Helsinki Conclusions' under the principle of peaceful settlement of disputes in accordance with the UN charter.

The 2006 Accession Partnership and the Negotiating Framework adopted a similar wording, though they no longer cited the Helsinki Conclusions which set the end of 2004 as the deadline for the submission of unresolved disputes to the jurisdiction of the International Court of Justice (ICJ). Instead, they referred to the jurisdiction of the ICJ without mentioning a deadline. Meanwhile, since 2000 every regular or progress report on Turkey has insisted on the resolution of border disputes, almost entirely with Greece, and since 2001 have dealt with this in a sub-section under the political criteria.[36]

On 28 May 2004, in a speech delivered at Oxford University, Turkish Prime Minister, Recep Tayyip Erdoğan, declared that 'if Turco-Greek rapprochement is possible today, it is because we have a common ground through which mutual perceptions are formed. That common ground is the EU.'[37] In this sense, Turkey's desire to enter the EU and the latter's policy of conditionality culminated in the Europeanisation of TFP towards Greece. In the same speech, Erdoğan also focused on a 'win–win approach' on the Cyprus issue, revealing a change in Turkey's position on what has been one of the major foreign policy issues since the 1960s. Indeed, instead of consolidating the status quo, Turkey's position on the Cyprus issue 'has been replaced with an active, solution-seeking behaviour' in the course of the last decade.[38]

In 2004, Turkey supported a 'yes' vote in the referendum on the Annan Plan on the unification of the island. In July 2005, Turkey adopted the Additional Protocol to extend the application of the Turkey–EU Customs Union to the new member states that acceded to the Union in 2004, though resisting its implementation in a manner that would allow Greek-Cypriot ships and aircrafts access to Turkish ports. Clearly, the Turkish stance on Cyprus over the last decade

---

[35]For this argument, see B. Rumelili, 'Civil society and the Europeanisation of Greek–Turkish cooperation', *South European Society and Politics*, 10, April 2005, pp. 45–56.

[36]Heading B.1.4 in the 2001 and 2002 reports, B.1.5 in the 2003 and 2004 reports, all under the title of 'Peaceful Settlement of Border Disputes'; B.1.3 in the 2005 report under the title of 'Regional Issues' with a sub-title of 'Peaceful Settlement of Border Disputes', and finally heading 1.2.3 in the 2006 report under the title of 'Regional Issues and International Obligations' with a sub-title of 'Peaceful Settlement of Border Disputes'.

[37]R. T. Erdoğan, 'Why the EU needs Turkey', http://www.sant.ox.ac.uk/esc/esc-lectures/Erdogan1.pdf.

[38]A. Tekin, 'The evolution of Turkish foreign policy: the impact of Europeanisation', *Workshop on EU–Turkey Relations: Opportunities, Challenges and Unknowns*, University of Pittsburgh, 17 November 2005.

has been heavily accentuated by its EU accession process. Through conditionality Turkey has been expected to:

> ensure continued support for efforts to find a comprehensive settlement of the Cyprus problem within the UN framework and in line with the principles on which the Union is founded, whilst contributing to a better climate for a comprehensive settlement; implement fully the Protocol adapting the Ankara Agreement to the accession of the 10 new EU Member States including Cyprus; and take concrete steps for the normalisation of bilateral relations with all Member States, including the Republic of Cyprus, as soon as possible.[39]

Failure to do so would surely cause delays in the course of negotiations or in the eventual membership, as seen at the end of 2006, when eight of the 35 negotiating chapters were suspended until Turkey admits Greek-Cypriot planes and ships to its ports.[40] This is a clear indication of the power and use of EU conditionality.

Although the Cyprus issue has created bitterness in EU–Turkey relations over the ports problem, Turkish policy on Cyprus has evolved from a more nationalist and confrontationist stance to one that accommodates options open to dialogue, cooperation, win–win solutions, activism and multilateralism. This is a novelty and without the EU accession process and membership prospect, Turkey would not have been in a position to initiate these kind of changes on such a sensitive foreign policy issue. Therefore, in both cases the winds of change have clearly resulted from the EU pressures, thereby allowing us to explain the substantial shift in TFP from the prism of Europeanisation through conditionality.

Conditionality through the CFSP *acquis*: EU-like Turkish foreign policy?

Conditionality in the CFSP chapter directs Turkey to progressively align with EU statements, and to apply sanctions and restrictive measures when and where required. In this respect, by fulfilling the CFSP requirements, TFP is increasingly coming closer to the foreign policy of the EU. This has been apparent in Turkey's progressive participation in military operations conducted under the framework of the European Security and Defence Policy (ESDP) and in its adoption of uncontroversial documents under the CFSP chapter, such as those related to terrorism. However, a snapshot of TFP towards the Middle East would show us a more complicated picture and reveal that EU conditionality is not the only factor explaining change.

In the course of the last decade, TFP towards the Middle East has moved in the direction of deepening economic ties through 'increased interdependence, restrained resort to military might and engagement with parties'.[41] This coincides

---

[39]'Council Decision of 23 January 2006 on the principles, priorities, intermediate objectives and conditions contained in the accession partnership with the Republic of Turkey 2006/35/EC', *Official Journal of the European Union*, L 22/34, 26 January 2006.

[40]M. Aydın, 'Cyprus: can burning bridges be a step towards peace?', *TEPAV Policy Brief*, 31 January 2007.

[41]Tekin, op. cit., p. 6.

with the EU's policy of tying the countries of the region to the Union through economic channels (e.g. trade agreements with most of the Middle Eastern countries) or engaging with the parties and acting as a mediator without taking sides (e.g. the EU as a part of the Quartet). Turkey's alignment to EU policy in the Arab–Israeli conflict did not happen automatically because the EU said so. Israel's alleged presence in northern Iraq and assistance to Kurdish *peshmerga*, coupled with the current Turkish government's pro-Palestinian sentiments, deflated the previously strategic relationship between Israel and Turkey and eased Turkey's move to a stand in between the Arabs and the Israelis, criticizing both and supporting the peace process with more deeds than rhetoric.[42]

In the case of Iran, Turkey has supported EU efforts to obtain long-term guarantees for the implementation of the Nuclear Non-Proliferation Treaty and its Nuclear Safeguards Agreement with the IAEA by Iran as well as the Union's proposals for a possible Trade and Cooperation Agreement with Iran.[43] However, here again, Turkey has aligned its policy to that of the Union, not primarily because the EU puts forward this as a condition but because of its own volatile relations with Iran. Turkey's growing trade relations,[44] as well as its need for Iran's natural gas and wish to avoid another war on its borders, prompted the Turkish authorities to opt for a non-military option which the EU is pursuing at the moment.

While Turkey's opposition to the war in Iraq and the fact it has refrained from mounting a major cross-border military operation against PKK bases in northern Iraq, in addition to its policy of supporting diplomacy rather than coercion in Iran, can be explained within the framework of foreign policy alignment with the Union, its policy towards the Iraqi war can also be explained by domestic pressures. Thus, although some of the changes in TFP have clearly originated from compliance with the CFSP *acquis*, it is difficult to pin those changes down with reference only to the EU process and without considering other variables.

Conclusion

After the Cold War, Turkey found itself surrounded by a series of conflicts, and realized that 'it may find itself facing military threats all around without the possibility to evoke the Western security umbrella for protection'.[45] Thus, changing geopolitical dynamics, diminishing European support, growing nationalism and awareness of ethnic issues in the world as well as in Turkey created a new type of foreign policy, which was characterized by a national security discourse and coercion towards opponents. For instance, in 1996 Turkey and Greece came to the brink of war over uninhabited rocky islets in the Aegean, followed by a Turkish declaration of 'Grey Zones'. A year before the Helsinki Council, Turkey threatened to use force against Syria. However, this era

---

[42]Kirişçi, op. cit., p. 63.

[43]See Chapter 31 of the 2006 Progress Report on Turkey, as well as M. Emerson and N. Tocci, 'Turkey as a bridgehead and spearhead: integrating EU and Turkish foreign policy', *EU–Turkey Working Papers*, 1, August 2004, p. 25.

[44]Between 2002 and 2004 bilateral trade rose from US$1.2 to US$2.3 billion per year. Turkey is the third largest investor in Iran. See Emerson and Tocci, ibid.

[45]M. Aydın, 'The determinants of Turkish foreign policy, and Turkey's European vocation', *The Review of International Affairs*, 3, Winter 2003, pp. 323–324.

of coercive attitudes appears to be over and TFP has been evolving since the Helsinki Summit of 1999.

Since then, Turkey's political and economic relations with the countries within its vicinity have been improved through an active, cooperative and constructive policy; using diplomacy and trade rather than coercion and pressure. Dialogue and a 'win–win' attitude have been mentioned frequently. In regional conflicts, rather than taking sides, Turkey has been adopting a balanced hands-off approach, coupled with mediation efforts and a role of trustworthy regional stabilizer. In other words, Turkey has moved to become a 'benign regional power', rather than a post-cold war warrior.[46]

Prospects for EU membership certainly played a role in this transformation and Europeanisation with its mechanism of conditionality provides a useful framework in analysing the shifts in TFP in the course of the last decade. When analysing the comparative effectiveness of the types of conditionality that have been employed in the Turkish case, there are clear indications that adherence to political criteria, whether *de jure* or de facto, incorporating democratisation and security/stability issues within the EU zone (e.g. relations with Greece or Cyprus), has been more relevant in transforming TFP than alignment to the CFSP (or conditionality through the CFSP *acquis*) that mainly involves policies towards extra-EU areas (e.g. relations with Armenia or the Middle Eastern states). In any case, apart from a few thorny areas, such as relations with Armenia, Turkey already complies with most of the CFSP *acquis* voluntarily so that the EU does not need to apply conditionality extensively. In comparing the *de jure* and de facto political criteria, on the other hand, it seems that the *de jure* application has been more effective than the de facto expansion of political criteria.

Nevertheless, an exclusive focus on conditionality and an analysis based solely on the Europeanisation perspective cannot provide a full explanation for the evolution of TFP since 1999. A more complete analysis would necessitate a broader approach, encompassing the effects of other relevant actors, both internal and external, to complement the impact of EU conditionality.

---

[46]Quoted from Oniş in Kirişçi, op. cit., p. 13.

Religiosity and protest behaviour: the case of Turkey in comparative perspective

ERSIN KALAYCIOĞLU

Since the 1960s, Turkey has experienced an increasing variety of political acts carried out to influence, hinder or protest decisions taken by the political authorities. As acts of protest, they have been quite unconventional in their methods and substance. Some have involved such violent actions as assassinations, suicides, bombings or lynching. Others have been less violent, but just as unconventional in their substance, including forceful occupations of buildings, stoppages of traffic on the city and intercity roads, wildcat strikes and boycotts. The latter were not always violent but they constituted unconventional forms of political behaviour, and some were also illegal. In the 1990s, those who claimed to act in the name of Islam and even Allah (God) began to perpetrate acts of political protest and violence in Turkey. The domestic and international notoriety of such acts has increased over the years, particularly given the issue of engagement with international terror networks such as al-Qaeda. Indeed, in November 2003, Turkey's most populous city, Istanbul, was rocked by four car bomb attacks to two synagogues, the British General Consulate and the HSBC bank.

Violent acts of unconventional political participation, such as those which have taken place in the USA and elsewhere since 11 September 2001, have fostered a debate over the role played by religiosity in precipitating acts of political protest. Recently, more specific arguments have been made supporting the view that Islam and Islamic beliefs act as a fount of political protest and violence. Although such claims seem to abound in the popular press in Europe and North America, the role of Islam in fostering political protest among Muslim communities has been scantly subject to systematic observation and study. There has been an abundance of studies of Islam as religious ideology and practice; plentiful studies of Islam as inspiration for political regime and practices; and even some studies of Islam as a source of anti-system, revolutionary movements and radicalism. It is a well-established fact that Islam has played a role in inspiring some to protest political decisions and political protest. However, we are still in the dark about the role Islam plays in precipitating protest potential among Muslim populations at large.

This paper aims to delve into the relatively understudied realm of religiosity as a motive for unconventional political participation and seeks to empirically establish the impact of religiosity on protest potential. The paper examines the sources or determinants of protest potential in the overwhelmingly Sunni Muslim society of Turkey. It aims to reveal the role played by Islamic religiosity in Turkey and to compare and contrast this with the role of religiosity as a determinant of protest potential in the overwhelmingly Christian societies of Europe.

Religiosity as a source of political protest in Muslim communities may best be assessed when it is considered from a theoretical perspective as an independent variable that influences protest potential. The method followed in this study is to measure the effect of religiosity vis-à-vis the other independent variables that may influence protest behaviour. Such an approach enables the researcher to make a relatively accurate assessment of how powerful religiosity is in comparison to other independent variables of a theory of protest behaviour. Secondly, the research findings will be compared with the results of other studies, which have measured and evaluated religiosity in Christian communities or societies of Europe and North America. Such a comparison offers insight into the extent to which being religious in Muslim communities accounts for protest behaviour, as opposed to 'religiousness' of any other kind, such as 'Christian religiosity' per se.

The changing political opportunity structure in Turkey

The opportunity structure of the Turkish political system has been influenced by the oscillating nature of the country's Constitutions, which have often vacillated between liberal and repressive regimes. In 1923–1945 Turkey hosted a one-party regime which, though pragmatic in nature, rarely left room for legitimate political opposition to form and function. However, general and local elections did take place and people were encouraged to take part in them, although the only choice they were offered was whether or not to support the list of candidates on the Republican People's Party (CHP) ticket. The plebiscitarian elections of the one-party era motivated people to take part in conventional political participation, but discouraged them from contestations of power through acts of protest. Indeed, the CHP elite tried to create 'mobilized participation' that was openly supportive of the government and regime, rather than countervailing forms of participation that contested the elites in power. The costs of protest participation were too stiff to bear for most. Despite this, there were protest acts and even outright rebellion in the 1920s and the 1930s. Such rebellion often involved armed uprisings. This was therefore more severe than the acts of protest participation, such as peaceful demonstrations, protest rallies, petitioning or picketing, which we are going to consider in this paper.

At the end of the Second World War came a swift and dramatic change in the Turkish political opportunity structure. Opposition parties were legally permitted to form and to participate in general elections, and the country moved toward multi-party democracy. Until 1960 the country experienced a contest between the Democrat Party (DP) and the CHP through free and fair elections. Interest group activities were still severely curtailed, and the DP governments often appealed to press censorship to muffle opposition. Nevertheless, in comparison to the one-party era, opportunities for mass participation increased. The Soviet threat and the ideological corollaries of neighbouring Russia (Marxism–Leninism, socialism and social democracy) were outlawed and frequently declared to be the major threat to public well-being. Interestingly enough, Islamic revivalists found a relatively liberal environment to spring back into action under DP rule. Religious groups began to appear at mass rallies and demonstrations and were treated with relative tolerance.

In 1960 Turkey experienced a major democratic breakdown as young officers carried out a military coup and took office. The new Constitution of 1961, which was drawn up by students of law and politics, was the most liberal democratic Constitution Turkey has ever adopted. It introduced many new institutions such as a Senate (upper chamber) of the Turkish Grand National Assembly, a Constitutional Court, a free press, an autonomous Turkish Radio and Television administration, and autonomy of the state universities. A dynamic interest group system began to emerge and function, as socialist, social democratic, national socialist and religious revivalist parties emerged and made their indelible marks on the Turkish political system. During this period, Turkey also began to experience rule by coalition governments. Unfortunately, the governments of the 1970s failed to improve the country's economic performance, social welfare and foreign relations. In the meantime, Turkey slid into chaos and political unrest. It looked as if a civil war might break out when in 1980, the military intervened once again, this time in an institutional coup, in which the top brass of the military assumed political authority and the institution of the armed forces took over the government.

In the 1960s and 1970s, conventional and unconventional participation increased by leaps and bounds.[1] On 1 May 1977, Turkey experienced repression of participation on an unprecedented scale. During the Labour Day Parade, the crowd was sprayed with bullets and bombs by unidentified perpetrators. Tens died and many more were wounded. The military coup put an end to all such developments.

The liberal regime of the 1961 Constitution, the idea of limited government, checks and balances between the branches of Turkish government, and the vigorous milieu of the interest groups were all blamed for the political instability of the late 1970s. The 1982 Constitution was designed not only to put the Turkish political system in order but also to provide the necessary tools for the government to deal effectively with political instability. If the 1961 Constitution stood for liberal democracy, the 1982 Constitution provided for law and order. The illiberal political regime of the 1982 Constitution established numerous constraints to control and channel political participation into conventional forms, such as voting, bureaucratic contacting, and public discussion of local and national issues. Party and interest group variety and scope of action were both restricted for a while. Consequently, the frequency and scope of voluntary actions and associability faded to a new nadir in Turkish politics.[2]

Then Turkey applied for European Community membership in 1987 and the Soviet Union collapsed on 31 December 1991. In the context of the country's new foreign economic and political relations and the post-Cold War international system, the 1982 Constitution looked increasingly out of date and out of touch with reality and with the new international relations of Turkey. From 1995 onwards, major steps were taken to amend the 1982 Constitution. The new political opportunity structure provides ample room for protest, although

---

[1] E. Kalaycıoğlu and I. Turan, 'Measuring political participation: a cross-cultural application', *Comparative Political Studies*, 14(1), 1981, pp. 123–135; E. Kalaycıoğlu, *Karşılaştırmalı Siyasal Katılma*, İstanbul Üniversitesi S. B. F. Pub., İstanbul, 1983.

[2] B. Toprak, 'Civil society in Turkey', in A. R. Norton (ed.), *Civil Society in the Middle East*, E. J. Brill, Leiden/New York/Köln, 1996, p. 104.

occasional assassinations and assassination attempts, bombings and terrorist incidents continue to test the tolerance of the political authorities. Nevertheless, Turkey has moved toward a much more liberal constitutional regime, which provides room for vigorous civil activism and for a wide array of political parties, including some regime-threatening ones. In December 2004 the EU Commission finally declared Turkey as having sufficiently met the political criteria for EU entry to start negotiations for full membership, which formally opened in October 2005.

Sources of political participation in Turkey

The changing nature of the Turkish opportunity structure has enabled anti-system interest groups and political parties to function with greater assertiveness in the Turkish political system. Racist and religious parties are still outlawed in Turkey, although many parties with clear ultra-nationalist and overtly Islamic tendencies have again been legally functioning since the 1980s. Religious interest groups used economic, cultural and social organizations as front operations to mask their religious solidarity networks. Indeed, religious organizations, in the form of mosque-building societies or Kur'anic schools, have become the most frequently established civil society associations, with relatively large numbers of members and gatherings. The zeal of the military government of 1980–1983 in summoning the help of religious brotherhoods to confront what it saw as an existential Marxist–Leninist challenge paved the way for the benign neglect of the former's successful penetration into the shanty towns in and around the major cities of Turkey. The idea of marrying Turkish nationalism with Sunni Islam, succinctly known as the 'Turkish Islamic Synthesis', was almost elevated to the level of official state ideology in the 1980s. Such practices obviously facilitated the growing role of Islam in Turkish society and politics.

Under the circumstances, the Sunni Muslim networks, underground religious orders and their legal front operations provided new channels for upward social mobility, social solidarity and political influence for the displaced rural masses who flocked to the major cities in search of education, jobs, health care and a better future. It has long been documented that urbanization functions as the root cause of political participation in Turkey and elsewhere.[3] Indeed, urbanization seems to have provided similar opportunities for formal education, better health care and other social welfare services in Turkey, while it has come to serve as a new training ground for militants of all kinds, including those of political Islam.[4] Therefore, both formal secular education, and religious associability and activism are promoted in the same social milieu of the metropolitan shanty towns of Turkey.

Two other background characteristics, age and gender, seem to have provided the fount out of which emerged such immediate determinants of political participation as interest in, information and knowledge about politics. A sense of being effective in influencing the decisions of political authorities often emerges from such background factors as well.[5] Unconventional forms of participation,

---

[3]D. Lerner, *Passing of the Traditional Society*, The Free Press, New York, 1958; Kalaycıoğlu, *Karşılaştırmalı*, op. cit., pp. 373–375.

[4]D. Shankland, *Islam and Society in Turkey*, Eothen Press, Walkington, 1999, pp. 95–104.

[5]E. Kalaycıoğlu, 'Unconventional political participation in Turkey and Europe: comparative perspectives', *IL POLITICO Facolta di Scienze Politiche Dell'Universita di Pavia*, No. 45, 1997, p. 63.

such as rallying, boycotts, building occupations, etc. require youthfulness. Such participation requires a considerable amount of physical strength and energy, and a psychological readiness to rebel, which is often easier during youth or even adolescence. Similarly, gender influences different attitudes towards politics. Women and girls tend to be socialized into 'domestic' roles, while childhood plays, stories and legends motivate Turkish boys to take part in 'out-of-home' activities. Families often provide similar cues and instruction to their young members. Consequently, women tend to be less motivated to follow, learn, and react to political events and developments in the country. Several studies have indicated that politics is still a 'male vocation' in Turkey, where women have a hard time taking part, even when they are highly motivated and ambitious. It is also a matter of fact that girls have less opportunity to advance in school, while some do not even enjoy much chance of attending.[6] So far as protest potential is concerned, it seems as if it is even harder for women to take part in such acts as boycotts, demonstrations and wildcat strikes, which often include the risk of getting involved in physical struggles with the police. Protest participation seems to be another domain where male members of society tend to be more motivated to take part.

Such background factors also help to determine the length of exposure to secular education and individual experiences. Lengthy formal and secular education often leads to low levels of religiosity, heightened feelings of political efficacy and an increased interest in politics.[7] Earlier studies indicated that lack of formal, secular education tended to be positively correlated with religiosity for the voting age population in Turkey.[8] The absence of a formal educational background seems to promote a feeling of powerlessness and lack of interest in the broader realms of political life.[9] Similarly, lengthy formal religious education should be expected to develop firm belief in religion, a deep sense of religiosity. In summary, there are solid grounds to expect that the length and type of formal education function as a major determinant of both religiosity and other political motives of protest participation.

In order to better appraise the role of religiosity in engendering protest behaviour, we need to assess its status among the variables mentioned in the preceding analysis. Andrian and Apter argue that religiosity provides for cultural power and 'symbolic capital', and also 'justif[ies] and criticize[s] the exercise of political power'.[10] Wallace and Jenkins argue that in post-industrial societies, the clash between secularized protesters and supporters of traditional religious morality plays an important role in explaining protest behaviour. They further suggest that in the consolidated democracies of Western Europe and the USA, religiosity consistently reduces protest potential. This is especially the case in Italy and Austria, where Catholics form a huge majority. Thus, Catholicism has

---

[6] E. Kalaycıoğlu and B. Toprak, *İş Yaşamı, Üst Yönetim ve Siyasette Kadın*, TESEV Yayınları, Istanbul, 2004, pp. 86–106; and Kalaycıoğlu, 'Unconventional political participation', ibid., pp. 40–48.

[7] A. Marsh and M. Kaase, 'Background of political action', in S. H. Barnes *et al.* (eds), *Political Action: Mass Participation in Five Western Democracies*, Sage, Beverley Hills and London, 1979, pp. 87–136.

[8] Kalaycıoğlu, 'Unconventional political participation', op. cit., p. 55.

[9] L. W. Milbrath and M. L. Goel, *Political Participation: How and Why Do People Get Involved in Politics?*, Rand McNally, Chicago, IL, 1977, p. 68.

[10] C. F. Andrian and D. E. Apter, *Political Protest and Social Change: Analyzing Politics*, University Press, New York, 1995, p. 60.

a significant negative effect on protest behaviour. Only in those countries where Catholics are a small minority are they protest prone.[11]

In a more recent study, Ronald Inglehart revealed that Islamic societies tend to adhere to traditional value orientations, and have a pronounced tendency to emphasise respect for authority.[12] If such a traditionalist tendency exists, then we should expect to find a relatively strong emphasis on obedience to authority and avoidance of protest. Overwhelmingly Muslim societies, just like overwhelmingly Catholic societies, would emerge as social settings where religion plays a major role in determining protest behaviour, through working *against* protest behaviour and potential.

Even though religiosity per se functions as a major source of political activism, it is only one motive among several that influence and determine protest potential. Unless examined as part of a web of influences, it is not possible to comprehend how important a role religiosity plays in determining protest potential in any specific political and social context. In fact, it is absolutely necessary to determine the relative strength and nature of the relationship between religiosity and protest potential, before developing a working hypothesis about the role of Sunni Islamic values and practices in fostering protest activity in a Muslim society. With this aim, a causal model was drawn up in which religiosity is employed as an endogenous variable, allowing us to estimate the strength and sign of the path coefficient between religiosity and protest potential (Figure 1).

The data-set

The data for the study were collected during the period 10–25 October 2002 through a field survey carried out in 100 sub-provincial districts (*ilçe*), located in 33 out of the 81 provinces (*il*) of Turkey. The survey sample was determined by means of multi-stage stratified cluster sampling of the sub-provinces. Face-to-face interviews were conducted with 2028 respondents, yielding a sample size with ±2.2 per cent sampling error. The refusal rates encountered during the fieldwork were 55 per cent on the first attempts and 35 per cent on the second. The interviews were conducted at the height of the 2002 election campaign.

Operationalization of the variables

The dependent variable: protest potential

Protest potential is operationalized by means of factor analysing the responses registered by the interviewees to the following five questions:

'Have you ever taken part, or would you consider taking part, in any of the activities listed below?

---

[11]M. Wallace and J. C. Jenkins, 'The new class, postindustrialism, and neocorporatism: three images of social protest in the Western democracies', in J. C. Jenkins and B. Klandermans (eds), *The Politics of Social Protest: Comparative Perspectives on States and Social Movements*, University of Minnesota Press, Minneapolis, 1995, pp. 110, 125.

[12]R. Inglehart, 'The worldviews of Islamic publics in global perspective', in M. Moaddel (ed.), *Worldviews of Islamic Publics*, Palgrave, New York, 2005, pp. 5–7.

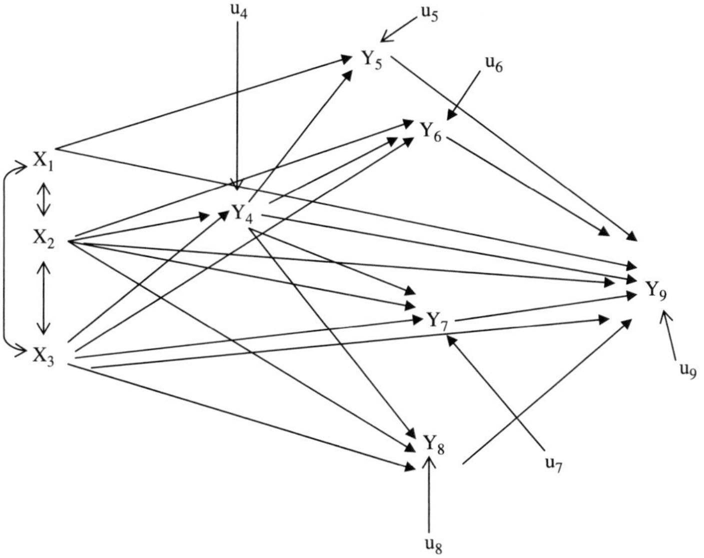

Simultaneous equations:

$$Y_9 = p_{91}X_1 + p_{92}X_2 + p_{93}X_3 + p_{94}Y_4 + p_{95}Y_5 + p_{96}Y_6 + p_{97}Y_7 + p_{8u8}Y_8 + p_{9u9}u_9.$$
$$Y_8 = p_{82}X_2 + p_{93}X_3 + p_{94}Y_4 + p_{8u8}u_8.$$
$$Y_7 = p_{72}X_2 + p_{73}X_3 + p_{84}Y_4 + p_{7u7}u_7.$$
$$Y_6 = p_{62}X_2 + p_{63}X_3 + p_{64}Y_4 + p_{6u6}u_6.$$
$$Y_5 = p_{51}X_1 + p_{54}Y_4 + p_{5u5}u_5.$$
$$Y_4 = p_{42}X_2 + p_{43}X_3 + p_{4u4}u_4.$$

Glossary of variables:

Y_9 = protest potential
Y_8 = political interest
Y_7 = political efficacy
Y_6 = political knowledge
Y_5 = religiosity
Y_4 = length of formal education
X_{34} = place of residence
X_2 = gender
X_1 = age

Figure 1. A general model of political participation (protest potential). *Sources*: Kalaycıoğlu, 1983, pp. 387–407; Kalaycıoğlu, 1997, p. 57.

1. Petitioning (*Toplu Dilekçe*)
2. Participation in boycotts
3. Participation in legal demonstrations
4. Participation in wildcat strikes
5. Occupation of buildings or offices.

The responses given to each of the above-listed questions ranged between 'participated', 'would consider participation' or 'would never consider participation'. The first category was assigned a numeral value of '3', the second category was assigned '2' and the last category was assigned the value of '1'.

Table 1. Protest potential (frequency distributions)

Potential action	Takes part in petitioning (%)	Takes part in boycott (%)	Takes part in legal demonstrations (%)	Takes part in wildcat strikes (%)	Takes part in occupation of buildings (%)
Never takes place (1)	68.8	81.4	77.3	90.5	93.3
May take place (2)	20.9	12.1	16.6	4.8	2.7
Took place (3)	6.6	3.2	3.3	1.2	0.6
Don't know/no response	3.8	3.3	2.8	3.5	3.3
Total percentage	100.0	100.0	100.0	100.0	100.0
Total observations	1984	1984	1984	1984	1984

The individual frequency distributions per variable mentioned above are presented in Table 1–7. The missing cases were omitted from further analysis. Then, the above-mentioned five variables were subjected to a principal components analysis and were all loaded on the principal (single) factor (see Table 2). The factor scores were then calculated from the principal factor loadings of the principal factor solution presented in Table 2.

The independent variables

Gender is operationalized by assigning '1' to female and '2' to male respondents in the sample. Age is measured by subtracting the birth dates registered by each respondent from the year 1997. Place of residence is operationalized by assigning the numeral '2' to city dwellers and '1' to inhabitants of rural settlements. The scale of education employed in this paper is designed to measure the length of exposure to formal, secular education in Turkey. Respondents who attend religious schools are thus assigned the numeral value of '−1', those with no schooling '0', while those with elementary to postgraduate school experience were assigned numeral values that ranged between '1' and '8'.

Attitudinal variables were operationalized by calculating factor scores that corresponded to two dimensions of religiosity, which I refer to as religious belief and religious traditionalism, through principal components factor analysis (see Table 3), and political interest, political efficacy and political knowledge (see Table 4). The factors extracted from the factor analysis were subjected to a varimax rotation, so that each dimension (variable) would be linearly independent of each other (see Tables 3 and 4). Therefore, in the following causal analysis we managed to avoid a concern with multicollinearity for those independent variables included in the preceding factor analysis exercise. The procedure used in operationalizing the attitudinal variables in this paper is the same as in the previous analysis of protest potential in Turkey.[13]

---

[13]Kalaycıoğlu, 'Unconventional political participation', op. cit., pp. 60–61.

Table 2. Protest potential: principal components analysis

Component matrix[a]	
Variables	Component Protest potential
Petitioning	0.746
Taking part in boycott	0.841
Taking part in legal demonstration	0.826
Taking part in wildcat strike	0.786
Taking part in occupation of building or place of work	0.656

Extraction method: principal component analysis.
[a]One component extracted.

Protest potential in Turkey

When the same model is applied to protest potential in Turkey, it performs almost as well as the conventional participation model (see Figure 2). Young male voters seem to be more inclined to take part in protest behaviour. Urbanization *per se* seems to provide fertile ground to fuel protest potential. Consequently, protest potential seems to be concentrated in the declining communities of the Turkish cities and among their young male inhabitants who are more ready to use the relatively risky and even illegal methods and means of political protest.

So far as the main focus of this paper is concerned, religiosity seems to have a sizable and dampening effect on protest potential. Islam as either faith or practice with overt political overtones does not seem to be positively correlated with protest behaviour. Pearson product–moment correlations between the factor scores of 'Islam as Faith' and 'Political Islam', as operationalized in this paper, and factor scores for protest potential are -0.29 and -0.14, and both are statistically significant at the 0.05 level of significance. Pious Muslims tend not to be inclined toward protest potential.

Radical Islamic groups have always existed in Turkish society, yet they have also been marginal to Turkish politics. In fact, when organized as political parties, they often failed to poll more than a few percentage points of the national vote unless and until they mellowed to a point of arguing that they stand for no more than 'democracy and conservatism'. Mainstream political Islam in Turkey has vied for power through conventional channels of political participation since the 1960s. In fact, political parties and interest groups overtly espousing Sunni Islamic values have been extremely successful in obtaining power in the Turkish Grand National Assembly and the cabinets of various Prime Ministers since the 1970s. Consequently, there seems to be a greater proclivity to penetrate the legitimate channels of influence through canvassing the vote and mobilizing voters at the polls, than through engaging in acts of protest. Such acts seem to be committed by those who feel politically less efficacious than those who engage in conventional acts of participation. Protest behaviour in Turkey seems to be enacted more out of desperation, and by those who do not seem to have much chance of having their say with the political authorities. Religiosity does not seem to condone such acts, which appear to be perceived as rebellious behaviour,

Table 3. Religiosity (Turkey, 2002)

	Religiosity as:	
	Faith	Political Islam
How frequently have you been praying during the last year?	0.411	**0.564**
Except for funeral processions, how frequently were you able to visit a mosque during the last year?	0.218	**0.425**
Disregarding how frequently you have been able to pray, do you consider yourself as religious?	0.348	**0.484**
During Ramadan all restaurants and cafés should be closed until the fast break	0.053	**0.675**
I would object to my daughter's marriage to a non-Muslim	0.198	**0.630**
I would consider enrolling my child in the Imam Hatip (preacher) High School	0.068	**0.742**
High schools should segregate boys and girls	−0.030	**0.643**
Colleges should permit women students to cover their heads	0.101	**0.591**
Believes in:		
God	**0.711**	0.071
Life after death	**0.764**	0.097
Devil	**0.584**	0.051
Existence of spirit	**0.765**	0.135
Heaven and hell	**0.848**	0.170
Sin	**0.798**	0.127
Would you like to see Turkey become a theocracy based upon Sharia?	−0.019	**0.483**

Extraction method: principal component analysis.
Rotation method: varimax with Kaiser normalization.

a view sanctioned by mainstream Sunni interpretations of Islam. We should also add that some forms of protest behaviour entail a relatively high risk of the perpetrator being incarcerated, injured or even killed in the clashes with the security forces. If pious voters get their way through the ballot box, why should they feel the need to take part in protest acts involving severe political, legal and even lethal risks?

This study also reveals that political motives still play a major role in determining the protest potential of individual voters. However, as noted above, political efficacy seems not to play a role among the political motives incorporated into our model. This should be taken as a sign of relative lack of power or a perception of the relative ineffectiveness of protest acts. It seems as if protest behaviour seems to be the road taken by those who feel relatively ineffective. The religious orders and their economic interests have become far too integrated in the national economy and politically powerful in Turkey to be

Table 4. Political motives

Rotated component matrix[a]

Items	Political knowledge	Component Political interest	Political efficacy
How interested in politics	0.160	**0.815**	0.133
Follow government activities	0.254	**0.470**	0.160
Interested in the ongoing election campaigns	0.001	**0.808**	0.233
How important that a certain party wins for your household income to increase	−0.037	0.055	**0.798**
How much of an impact will your vote have on the outcome of 3 November 2002 elections	0.058	0.080	**0.770**
Party that can bring a major solution to a pressing problem exists	0.068	0.188	**0.585**
Know important issues of the campaign	**0.428**	**0.423**	−0.083
Knows when the Cyprus intervention took place	**0.657**	0.293	−0.090
Knows when the European Union accepted Turkey as an eligible candidate for full membership	**0.396**	0.290	−0.143
Knows the name of the minister in charge of the economy who was invited to run the austerity programme from his job at the World Bank	**0.677**	0.067	0.070
The name of the party and its leader that are reputed to lead according to the pollsters	**0.632**	−0.072	0.198

Extraction method: principal component analysis.
Rotation method: varimax with Kaiser normalization.
[a]Rotation converged in six iterations.

considered as desperate souls. Such religious orders show considerable ability in engaging and successfully lobbying the country's political authorities through democratic channels of influence. Thus, under the Turkish democratic regime, political Islam seems to enjoy many opportunities to exert influence effectively through established channels of conventional political participation. In contrast, an individual may take part in such acts as occupations or wildcat strikes, when s/he has the impression that conventional acts will not be sufficient to bring what s/he deserves. As we have revealed, participation in protests is correlated with being informed about politics and having a deep interest in political life. Those who lack interest and information about politics do not seem to become protest participants in Turkey (see Figure 2). Protestors are politically interested and informed individuals, who try to register their objections to political decisions through protests, not because such acts are more effective, but because they fail to influence the political authorities through any other means, or they believe that

Table 5. Determinants of political participation in Turkey (protest potential) (1990, 1996–1997, 2002)

Independent variables	Protest potential (1990)	Protest potential (1996–1997)	Protest potential (2002)
Gender	**0.08**	**0.10**	**−0.09**
Age	**−0.03***	**−0.05**	**−0.09**
Residence (urban/rural)	n/a	n/a	0.00
Formal secular education	0.15	0.21	0.05*
Political knowledge	n/a	n/a	0.13
Political efficacy	−0.09	−0.15	0.00
Political interest	0.15	0.28	0.17
Religiosity	−0.15	−0.36	−0.26
Number of cases	(980)	(1248)	(844)
R	0.47	0.64	0.41
R^2	0.23	0.41	0.17

Sources: Kalaycıoğlu, 1997, p. 62; Turkish Values Survey of 1996/7; Political Participation Survey 2002.
*Statistically not significant at $p < 0.05$ level of significance.
n/a = not applicable.
Table entries are direct influences by path coefficients, unless they are otherwise designated.

through protests they can get the attention of the media and put their issue on the political agenda.

The causal model used here seems to have slightly less explanatory power than the same model used in the previous studies in 1990 and 1997 (see Table 5). The direct influence of formal secular education on protest potential seems to have been completely eroded. However, formal secular education still plays a critical role in determining political motives, which in turn, play a major role in determining protest potential.

The role that religiosity and political interest play in determining protest potential seems also to have become well pronounced over the years in Turkey (see Table 5). The main reason for such a diminished influence of some of the critical variables as measured in 2002 seems to be the decreased variance in the dependent variable. For a while in the early 2000s, the PKK, the Maoist Kurdish terror movement, became less influential after its leader, Abdullah Öcalan, was captured in 1999. Similarly, in the aftermath of 11 September 2001, religious groups bent upon wreaking havoc in the country somewhat subsided, in particular after the forceful submission of the Hizbullah terror network in Turkey (unrelated to those of Iran or Lebanon) in 2001 (see Table 5). In fact, spatiotemporal comparison of the Turkish data seems to indicate that protest potential has decreased from the 1990s to 2002 (see Table 5).

A comparison of the Turkish data with similar findings from consolidated democracies in Europe and North America indicates that in the 1990s, Turkey used to lag behind only in terms of legal demonstrations and petitioning (see Table 6). In terms of boycotts, wildcat strikes and occupations, Turkish participation rates were low, but not the lowest (see Table 6). It is interesting

Table 6. Comparative protest potential in consolidated democracies and Turkey (percentage of those who recall participation in the corresponding acts)

Countries	Unconventional acts of political participation				
	Petitioning (%)	Boycotts (%)	Legal demonstrations (%)	Wildcat strikes (%)	Occupation of buildings (%)
Austria	45.5	4.8	9.8	1.0	0.7
Belgium	44.5	8.3	21.2	5.7	3.6
Britain	**74.5**	13.2	13.6	9.6	2.4
Denmark	50.3	10.2	27.0	**16.7**	2.0
France	51.4	11.3	31.2	9.4	**7.2**
Germany (West)	55.1	9.2	19.5	2.1	1.0
Iceland	46.6	**21.1**	23.4	*0.1*	1.3
India	22.4	15.2	15.3	5.4	0.7
Italy	44.2	10.0	**34.1**	5.6	7.0
Netherlands	50.1	8.4	25.0	2.5	3.1
Portugal	24.8	*3.5*	19.2	3.1	1.4
Spain	17.5	4.7	21.2	5.7	2.4
Sweden	69.9	15.8	21.8	2.9	*0.2*
USA	70.1	17.4	15.1	4.4	1.8
Turkey (1990)	*12.8*	5.2	*5.3*	1.4	1.2
Turkey (1997)	*13.5*	6.3	*6.1*	2.0	0.5
Turkey (2002)	6.8	3.3	3.4	1.3	0.6

Sources: World Values Survey (1989–1991); Turkish Values Surveys (1990 and 1996); Turkish Political Participation Survey 2002.
The figures in bold are the highest percentages per column and the figures in italics are the lowest.

to note that in the 1990s those acts of protest, such as petitioning and legal demonstrations, that might have been tolerated by the authorities did not seem to occur frequently. However, acts which did not have much chance of being perceived as legitimate by the political authorities, such as boycotts, wildcat strikes and occupations seem to have attracted more involvement in the early 2000s. As noted above, protest behaviour in Turkey took the form of negation or contestation of the political system, rather than legal objections to political decisions. Once anti-system movements lost their attraction, protest potential seems to have rapidly eroded in the early 2000s.

In determining protest potential in Turkey, religiosity plays a major role but a constellation of political resources (e.g. youthfulness, urban lifestyle, education) and motives (e.g. interest in politics, level of information about politics) are also influential (see Table 7). The research findings seem to coincide with the predictions of the working hypothesis: that *in overwhelmingly Muslim societies, protest potential is deeply influenced by religiosity, and religiosity reduces protest behaviour and potential.* The increasing success of overtly religious parties at the polls could also be considered as another factor mitigating the importance of Islamic activism in protesting the secular democratic order in Turkey.

Table 7 indicates that similar factors are also at play in the consolidated democracies of Europe and North America, as well as in Turkey, in determining the protest potential of individual voters (see Table 7). An examination of

Table 7. Multiple regression analysis of protest potential scales

(a) Countries

Variables	France	UK	USA	Germany	Turkey		
					1990	1996	2002
Age	−0.28	−0.29	−0.29	−0.25	−0.01*	−0.05	−0.01*
Sex/gender	0.18	0.21	0.16	0.14	0.09	0.12	0.11
Education	0.26	0.13	0.26	0.14	0.34	0.38	0.20
Strength of party identification	0.23	0.11	0.06	0.08	0.00*	0.12	−0.04*[a]
Political efficacy	n/a	0.13	0.10	0.22	0.11	−0.10	0.02*
Policy dissatisfaction	0.11	0.16	0.15	0.07	−0.09	−0.12	−0.04*[b]
R	0.58	0.50	0.56	0.50	0.41	0.50	0.26
R^2	0.34	0.25	0.31	0.25	0.16	0.25	0.07

(b) Countries

Variables	Netherlands	UK	USA	Germany	Austria	Turkey		
						1990	1996	2002
Age	−0.19	−0.28	−0.33	−0.25	−0.16	−0.04	−0.02*	−0.03*
Sex/gender	−0.09	−0.12	−0.04	−0.09	−0.11	−0.08	−0.13	0.15
Education	0.15	0.10	0.20	0.18	0.16	0.21	0.30	0.10
Religiousness	0.17	0.03	0.12	0.12	0.07	n/a	n/a	−0.19
Trade union membership	−0.03	−0.09	−0.04	−0.06	−0.03	−0.18	0.18	n/a
Occupational prestige	0.01	0.06	0.04	0.01	0.09	0.09	n/a	n/a
R	0.39	0.41	0.48	0.42	0.34	0.47	0.49	0.30
R^2	0.15	0.16	0.23	0.18	0.12	0.22	0.24	0.09

Sources: Marsh and Kaase, 1979, p. 131; Dalton, 1988, pp. 69–70; Kalaycıoğlu, 1997, pp. 67–68; Ali Çarkoğlu, Üstün Ergüder and Ersin Kalaycıoğlu, Political Participation Survey, 2002.
*Statistically not significant at 0.05 level of significance.
All table entries are standardized partial regression coefficients, except 'R' and 'R^2', which are the Pearson product–moment multiple correlation coefficients and determination coefficients for those independent variables and the dependent variable in the upper rows of each part of the table. The last three columns of the table on Turkey are my calculations from the Turkish Values Survey of 1990 and 1996, and from the 2002 participation and election study, the data of which are used in this paper (Kalaycıoğlu, 1997, p. 68).

the multiple correlation (R) and determination (R^2) coefficients in Table 7 indicates that the explanatory power of comparable models of unconventional political participation in consolidated democracies and Turkey are also quite similar. It seems as if the causal model employed in this study, which purports to explain protest potential as a consequence of political opportunities, resources and motives, seems to have relatively general applicability among democracies.

Conjectures and conclusions

Political participation in Turkey has incorporated a widening variety of acts over the years. Such acts of conventional political participation as voting, campaigning, contacting political authorities, and debating, discussing and deliberating political issues with the intention of finding solutions, have been employed by a large segment of the voting age population in the multi-party era. Protest potential, culminating in unconventional acts of participation in politics, has shown a trend towards increasing frequency and variety over the years. Petitions, boycotts, legal demonstrations and wildcat strikes were all on the increase throughout the 1990s, while potentially violent acts such as occupations were on the decrease. In the 2000s, protest potential in Turkish politics seems to have ebbed.

It is possible to explain political participation by reference to factors in Turkey that are similar to consolidated democracies in Europe and the USA. However, a large proportion of variation in political participation is still left unexplained in all of the political systems considered in this paper. It is possible to suspect that culturally or politically specific factors contribute to the unexplained variation in political participation. For example, in Turkey cultural impediments to political activism persist. Past research indicated that imbalances in political resource procurement, such as lack of formal education, income, occupation, etc., feed into, and in return, are fed back by patronage networks.[14] The relative lack of influence of attitudes on levels of political participation in Turkey is also due to the rampant practice of 'mobilized participation', especially among women and the rural poor. Although it may be easier to alter the opportunity structure through new legislation, it is much more difficult to change income distribution, employment practices and culture.

The preceding data analysis indicates that Islamic values and religiosity seem to play a major role in determining political protest in Turkey, by forestalling rather than fostering it. It is important to note that protest activities are popularly considered in Turkey to be futile acts, with little or no chance of getting a demand satisfied.[15] In contrast, religious interest groups have been quite successful in lobbying governments and the Turkish Grand National Assembly. They have also been quite successful in establishing powerful links with a variety of political

---

[14]C. Nurhat, 'Türkiye Köylerinde Olağandışı Oy Verme', *Ankara Üniversitesi Siyasal Bilgiler Fakültesi Dergisi*, XXVI(1), 1973, pp. 219–244; S. Sayari, 'Some notes on the beginnings of mass political participation', in E. Akarlı and G. Ben-Dor (eds), *Political Participation in Turkey: Historical Background and Present Problems*, Boğaziçi University Pub., Istanbul, 1975, pp. 121–133; A. Kutad, 'Patron–client relations: the state of the art and research in Eastern Europe', in E. Akarlı and G. Ben-Dor (eds), *Political Participation in Turkey: Historical Background and Present Problems*, Boğaziçi University Pub., Istanbul, 1975, pp. 61–87; E. Özbudun, *Türkiye'de Sosyal Değişme ve Siyasal Katılma*, Ankara Üniversitesi Hukuk Fakültesi Pub., Ankara, 1975, *passim*; E. Özbudun, 'Turkey', in J. M. Landau *et al.* (eds), *Electoral Politics in the Middle East: Issues, Voters, and Elites*, Croom Helm, London, 1980, *passim*.

[15]F. Adaman and A. Çarkoğlu, *Türkiye'de Yerel ve Merkezi Yönetimlerde Hizmetlerden Tatmin, Patronaj İlişkileri ve Reform*, TESEV, Istanbul, 2000, p. 67.

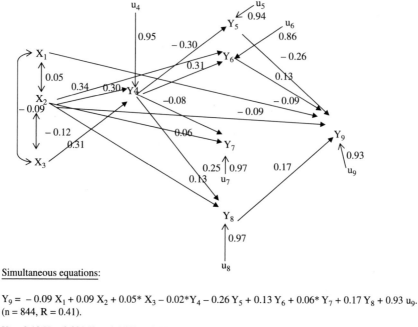

Simultaneous equations:

$Y_9 = -0.09 X_1 + 0.09 X_2 + 0.05^* X_3 - 0.02^* Y_4 - 0.26 Y_5 + 0.13 Y_6 + 0.06^* Y_7 + 0.17 Y_8 + 0.93 u_9.$
(n = 844, R = 0.41).

$Y_8 = 0.13 X_2 + 0.02^* X_3 + 0.25 Y_4 + 0.97 u_8.$
$Y_7 = 0.06 X_2 - 0.02^* X_3 - 0.08 Y_4 + 0.97 u_7.$
$Y_6 = 0.34 X_2 - 0.02^* X_3 + 0.31 Y_4 + 0.86 u_6.$
$Y_5 = 0.09 X_2 - 0.30 Y_4 + 0.94 u_5.$
$Y_4 = 0.30 X_2 + 0.31 X_3 + 0.95 u_4.$

Glossary of variables:

Y_9 = protest potential
Y_8 = political interest
Y_7 = political efficacy
Y_6 = political knowledge
Y_5 = religiosity
Y_4 = length of formal education
X_3 = place of residence
X_2 = gender
X_1 = age

Figure 2. A general model of political participation (protest potential) (Turkey, 2002).
Note: Only those paths that are empirically determined to exist are shown in the causal model.
*Statistically not significant at $p < 0.05$ level.

parties and influencing the selection of parliamentary deputies and cabinet ministers. Indeed, it has been argued since the 1990s that contemporary Islamist movements (in Turkey) thus appeared at the 'Centre' not only in the geographical sense of urban spaces, but also in the cultural and political sense of participation in the production of the symbols and values, and in the course of change.[16]

---

[16]N. Göle, 'Authoritarian secularism and Islamist politics: the case of Turkey', in A. R. Norton (ed.), *Civil Society in the Middle East*, E. J. Brill, Leiden and New York, 1996, p. 38.

In terms of political motives and the utilization of political resources that influence their political decisions, Turkish voters—religious communities included—seem to have accumulated a relatively high level of awareness, skills and knowledge. They seem to use such skills proficiently and effectively. Hence, such a citizenry enables the functioning of a vigorous multi-party system in Turkey. A culture of pluralism has gained enough ground in Turkey to enhance the sustainability of a democratic order. Religiosity does not seem to pose a major challenge, even though at times, various small and yet well-organized religious communities and groups have clashed with the political authorities, other communities and sects in Turkey. In conclusion, the findings of this paper indicate that such rebellious activity and protest behaviour stemming from religiosity (Sunni Islam) in Turkey seems to be more of an exception rather than the rule.

Turkish identity on the road to the EU: basic elements of French and German oppositional discourses

HAKAN YILMAZ

Identifying a collectivity consists of producing a series of rational arguments, emotional judgments and aesthetic choices with the purpose of distinguishing that particular collectivity from the others. Each collective identification is, therefore, an exercise in boundary drawing, separating the insiders from the outsiders, 'us' from 'them' and 'we' from 'the others'. Some recent studies on European identity have shown that Turkey is treated as an 'other' in the mental maps of many Europeans. Hence, according to an important cross-country qualitative study on European identity, carried out on behalf of the European Commission, the respondents have drawn a clear line between those countries that they believe form an 'integral part' of Europe and those that do not:

> The attitudes observed in France, Belgium, Luxembourg, Germany and Austria present relatively similar traits. As in the countries of the South of Europe, the idea comes across that there is a sort of moral duty to admit countries which historically and culturally form an integral part of Greater Europe and with which one's country has in the past sometimes had just as strong ties as with certain existing Member States.... However, the candidacy of Turkey is much more problematic in this regard and even raises absolute opposition.[1]

In recent years, identity-based arguments opposing Turkey's accession to the EU have been loudest and strongest in France and Germany, compared to the other major EU member countries. As we shall see below in the Eurobarometer surveys, in both countries public opposition to Turkey's EU membership has been much higher than the EU25 average. In both France and Germany, leading centre-right parties—the Union for a Popular Movement (UMP) in France and the Christian Democratic parties (CDU/CSU) in Germany—have officially positioned themselves against Turkish EU membership, on the grounds that Turkey is not a European country. Instead, they have proposed what they called a 'privileged partnership'. The UMP-dominated French parliament went so far as to pass a constitutional amendment, subjecting Turkey's EU membership to a public referendum. Turkey became one of the hottest issues during the French debates around the European Constitutional Treaty in late 2004 and early 2005, so much so that in the rhetoric of many French politicians saying no to Turkey and saying

---

[1]OPTEM, *Perceptions of the European Union: A Qualitative Study of the Public's Attitudes to and Expectations of the European Union in the 15 Member States and the 9 Candidate Countries*, prepared for the European Commission, 2001, p. 141. Available online at <http://ec.europa.eu/public_opinion/quali/ql_perceptions_summary_en.pdf>.

no to the EU Constitution became intractably linked. Some right-wing groups based in France, calling themselves 'European Citizens' Resistance Campaign', even started a campaign to 'Cross Turkey off the Euro Map'. 'Turkey is not part of the European bloc by any stretch of imagination, be it on sociological, historical, geographical, cultural, political, or religious grounds', argued the campaign leaders. They called upon the European citizens to show their opposition to Turkey 'by marking Turkey with a red cross on all your banknotes, in the bottom right-hand corner of the map of Europe at the verso of every Euro'. They did not forget to add that 'your banknotes remain legal tender which cannot be refused!'[2]

The main line dividing the pro-Turkish and anti-Turkish positions among the political elites in both France and Germany appears to be the left–right axis. Those who have actively supported, or have at least in principle agreed to, Turkey's EU accession have generally come from the left of the political spectrum. Those who have adopted a negative or an altogether exclusionist position have usually been found among the ranks of the right-wing parties, particularly of radical and extremist varieties. There are some exceptions to this rule, though, the most notable being the generally pro-Turkish stance of the former right-wing French president, Jacques Chirac. Right-wing conceptions of European identity by French and German elites today, and Turkey's place in those identity constructions, will be the focus of this paper. I will begin by evaluating the basic results of some pan-European opinion polls, showing how they reflect current French and German public attitudes towards Turkey.

I will then move on by exploring the constituent elements of the anti-Turkey discourses of the right-wing political and intellectual elites in France and Germany. Finally, I will examine the issue of Islam in general and the question of the headscarf in particular, showing how they shape the negative public image of Turkey in France and Germany.

This paper is the first product of a long-term research project on the identity dimensions of French and German attitudes towards EU–Turkey relations. The project reviewed recently published popular and scholarly books, journal articles, newspaper commentaries and other printed material on Turkey, including the transcripts of the parliamentary debates devoted to the issue of EU–Turkey relations. In addition to the printed material, some 11 websites and Internet discussion groups, partly or wholly devoted to the issue of Turkey, were examined. Finally, in autumn and winter 2005, 25 interviews were conducted with political and intellectual elites in France and Germany, who were asked to give both their own opinions and their evaluations of the intellectual milieu in their countries regarding the cultural dimensions of Turkey's integration with the EU.

'Turkey, the disliked country': evidence from the polls

Hrant Dink, the Armenian-Turkish journalist who recently lost his life in a terrorist attack in Istanbul, said at a conference on EU–Turkish relations that, at the emotional level, what was binding the European Union and Turkey together was not love but fear. What he meant by this was that the two sides did not have any particular willingness to live together, but could not separate their ways

---

[2]See <http://uk.rayezlaturquie.com>.

either, out of the fear that the costs of divorce would be greater than the costs of marriage.[3] A similar opinion was voiced by Marc Galle, a former member of the European Parliament and co-chair of the EU–Turkey Joint Parliamentary Committee in the early 1990s, who wrote a book entitled *Turkey, the Disliked Country*.[4]

A number of opinion polls conducted in Turkey and Europe have yielded data that lend support to the views of Dink and Galle. Hence, in a survey conducted in mid-2006 by the US-based Transatlantic Trends, people in nine selected EU member states (UK, France, Germany, Netherlands, Italy, Poland, Portugal, Slovakia and Spain) were asked to rank certain countries on the basis of how much 'affection' they feel for them, with '0' signifying no affection and '100' full affection. Among the nine EU member states included in the survey, Turkey happened to be one of the least liked countries with an average 'affection grade' of 42, above only Palestine (38) and Iran (28). For example, Germany's affection rate for Turkey was 43 (at about the European average) and France's was 38 (well below the European average). European affections towards Israel (43), China (46) and Russia (47) remained low but still above that for Turkey.[5]

One concrete result of the apparent lack of affection for Turkey on the part of the European publics is that Turkey is the least wanted country when it comes to EU Enlargement, even ranking below some Balkan countries, such as Serbia, which have only been given 'potential candidate' status. According to a Eurobarometer poll taken in the spring of 2006, when asked if they would oppose or support Turkey's membership in the EU once Turkey complies with all the conditions set by the European Union, close to 50 per cent of the respondents in EU25 said they would be on the opposing side, while the supporters remained at about 40 per cent. German opponents to Turkey's EU entry reached a record level of about 70 per cent while French opposition to Turkey remained at the high figure of nearly 55 per cent. Only 27 per cent of the German and approximately 40 per cent of the French respondents said they would be in favour of extending EU membership to Turkey.[6]

Basic elements of right-wing oppositional discourse on Turkey

Right-wing political elites usually draw upon pre-modern notions to define European identity today. From their perspective, three major constituents of European identity appear to be geography, history and religion. Geography is epitomized in the well-known attempts to draw the definitive territorial boundaries, borders or frontiers of Europe. It is worth noting here that, in the

---

[3]H. Dink, 'Minority rights in Turkey on the road to the EU', speech delivered at the conference Fourth Bogazici Student Meeting on the Process of Accession Negotiations between the EU and Turkey, organized by the Student Forum of Bogazici University's Centre for European Studies, Bogazici University, Istanbul, 22 December 2006.

[4]M. Galle, *Sevilmeyen Ülke Türkiye [Turkey, the Disliked Country]*, Bilgi Yayinevi, Ankara, 1995.

[5]Transatlantic Trends, *Top Line Data 2006* (fieldwork coordinated by TNS Opinion, interviews conducted 5–24 June 2006). Available online at <www.transatlantictrends.org>.

[6]European Commission, *Special Eurobarometer 255/Wave 65.2, Attitudes towards European Union Enlargement* (fieldwork: March–May 2006; publication: July 2006). Available online at <http:// europa.eu.int/comm/public_opinion/index_en.htm>.

cross-country study on European identity mentioned above, whenever the respondents used the term 'geography', they meant to exclude certain peoples and countries from Europe: 'When geography is mentioned … it is to exclude countries or areas … i.e. Russia … and, by extension, Ukraine and Belarus. Turkey is also often spontaneously considered to be non-European.'[7] Geography, as it appears from the OPTEM study, has become an essentially exclusionary device in the popular political culture of today's Europe. Boundaries, in other words, are drawn with the purpose of excluding certain peoples, marked as outsiders and others, rather than including them. History is sometimes understood as encompassing the classical or pre-medieval 'dawn' of modern European civilization that can be traced back to ancient Greece and Rome; sometimes it is construed as referring to Europe's post-Roman past rooted in medieval feudalism. Finally, religion is often thought of as consisting solely of Christianity, which time and again is taken to be a uniform whole without regard to its many internal divisions. A second, and post-Second World War, connotation of Europe's religious tradition is conceptualized as the 'Judeo-Christian' tradition, adding the Jewish tradition to the Christian one and positioning both against Islam.

Geographical, historical and religious arguments with the purpose of proving that Turkey does not belong to Europe and therefore has no place in the EU, can be found in abundance in the statements of right-wing French and German politicians in recent years. This type of categorical exclusionism of Turkey, on the basis of its 'cultural incompatibility' with Europe, can be found in the words of two well-known extreme right-wing politicians: Philippe De Villiers, currently head of the MPF (Movement for France) party, and Michael Glos, who was Chairman of the Christian Social Union Caucus in the German Bundestag in 2001. 'Turkey is not European', De Villiers said on the MPF website, 'neither by its history, nor by its geography, nor by its culture.'[8] Europe, according to De Villiers, must once and for all determine its borders. This determination must not be arbitrary but be based on the

> recognition of its roots, of the great civilising experiments which constituted it. And, there is nothing to be ashamed of our roots and no need to open up the 'Christian Club' to the outsiders, as if multiculturalism were our only future.[9]

Similarly, Michael Glos, in a 2001 article entitled 'Is Turkey Ready for Europe?', claimed that fulfilling the political and economic Copenhagen criteria were not enough to judge a country's European credentials. In his view, a country must also comply with the 'cultural criteria' of EU membership:

> In accepting new candidates we must expect them not only to meet the criteria laid down in Copenhagen, but also to integrate easily into the European cultural context.… precisely this capability is in doubt in the case of Turkey, a country which belongs to a different political and cultural sphere.[10]

---

[7]OPTEM, 2001, op. cit., p. 7.

[8]P. De Villiers, 'La Turquie dans l'Europe? Dix raisons de dire non!', 13 October 2006. Available online at <http://www.pourlafrance.fr/actualites_detail.php?id_com = 354>.

[9]De Villiers, 2006, op. cit.

[10]M. Glos, 'Is Turkey ready for Europe?', *Internationale Politik (Transatlantic Edition)*, 2(1), Spring 2001. Available online at <http://www.dgap.org/english/tip/tip0101/glos.html>.

Perhaps the most well-known cultural exclusionism vis-à-vis Turkey was that of Valéry Giscard d'Estaing, the former French President and Chair of the Convention on the Future of Europe. In an interview with the French newspaper *Le Monde* in November 2002, a month before the Copenhagen summit of the European Council, that was expected to take a decision regarding the opening of accession negotiations with Turkey, d'Estaing said that admitting Turkey 'would be the end of the European Union', because Turkey 'has a different culture, a different approach, a different way of life … Its capital is not in Europe, 95 percent of its population live outside Europe, it is not a European country.'[11] This line of argumentation can be found, more recently, in statements made by the new French President, Nicolas Sarkozy, during the 2007 election campaign:

> Turkey is not a European country, and as such she does not have a place inside the European Union. A Europe without borders would be the death of the great idea of political Europe. A Europe without borders is to condemn her to become a sub-region of the United Nations. I simply do not accept it.[12]

In similar vein, several years earlier, Edmund Stoiber, minister-president of the German state of Bavaria and chairman of the Christian Social Union (CSU), said it must be recognized that Europe as an entity has geographic limits which do not extend to the Turkey–Iraq border.[13] Turkish political and intellectual elites usually take pride in the notion that Turkey is a bridge between the East and the West, connecting Asia to Europe. In the eyes of Turkish leaders, this is a reason for the EU to include Turkey. According to the then CDU leader and now German Chancellor, Angela Merkel, on the other hand, this is a good reason for not making Turkey a full member of the EU: ' … a bridge … should never belong totally to one side. Turkey can fulfil its function of a bridge between Asia and Europe much better if it does not become a full member of the EU.'[14] Friedbert Pflüger, a leading member of the Christian democratic group in the German parliament, claimed that by taking Turkey in, the EU would cease to be a 'European' organization and would turn into a 'European-Asia Minor Union'. Challenging the ideas of his social democratic and Green opponents, Pflüger said that democracy, human rights and similar political values are not enough to define a specifically European identity:

> A political union needs something like a we-feeling. This we-feeling is something more than a commitment to democracy and human rights. It has to do with a centuries-old shared history: Greek antiquity, Roman law, the conflict between the Pope and the German Kaiser in the Middle Ages, the Reformation, the Enlightenment, all these that give Europe its specific character.[15]

---

[11]K. B. Richburg, 'Giscard declares Turkey too "different" to join EU', *Washington Post Foreign Service*, 9 November 2002. Available online at <http://www.washingtonpost>.

[12]N. Sarkozy, 'Je veux que l'Europe change', *Official Web Site of the UMP*, 21 February 2007. Available online at <http://www.u-m-p.org/site/index.php/ump/s_informer/discours/je_veux_que_l_europe_change>.

[13]B. O'Rourke, 'EU: Stoiber's remarks on "limits" to Europe touch sensitive nerve', *RFE/RL*, 9 December 2002. Available online at <http://www.rferl.org/nca/features/2002/05/21052002082330.asp>.

[14]Speech by A. Merkel, German Parliament, plenary debate on Turkey–EU relations, 16 December 2004. Available online at <www.bundestag.de>.

[15]Deutscher Bundestag, 16 December 2004, ibid.

'Extinguished volcano' is perhaps a good metaphor to understand the importance of Christianity in the discourses of the right-wing political elites of both France and Germany regarding European identity. The volcano has long stopped its activity but it is still there, it serves as a place marker, and perhaps one day it will start to erupt again. No mainstream right-wing politician today claims that a good European must also be a good, active, practising Christian. However, although no longer actively practised by the large majority of the European population, Christianity or rather sharing a common Christian heritage still serves for many right-wing political leaders as an identity marker. This sets Europeans (or 'true Europeans') apart from non-Europeans (or 'false Europeans' and 'new-born Europeans'). Christianity is understood not so much as a belief system or a theology but as a civilizational idea, political culture and lifestyle. As such, for example, it is believed that the cultural roots of some fundamental secular European values, such as the separation of spiritual and worldly affairs, the separation between the public and the private spheres, the idea of natural rights protecting the individual against the state, and, following Max Weber, the culture of capitalism, all have their roots in Europe's Christian heritage.

Hence, at a March 2007 press conference to mark the signature of the Declaration of Berlin, commemorating the 50th anniversary of the founding of the European Economic Community, German Chancellor, Angela Merkel, representing the presidency of the EU, said that 'the Judeo-Christian values … sustain the EU' and that 'we are marked by this Judeo-Christian past'.[16] In a February 2007 interview with the German news weekly *Focus*, Merkel stressed the importance she attached to Europe's common Christian values: 'No one doubts that they significantly shape our life, our society. I wonder, can we maintain the formative aspects of Christianity for day-to-day politics if the political sphere does not stand by them?'[17] Agustín José Menéndez, in an article entitled 'Christian Values and European Identity', argues critically that for a number of well-known European constitutional lawyers of pro-Christian orientations, Christianity, or rather Catholicism, lies at the basis of 'the most fundamental ethical values' and the 'common constitutional traditions' of European nations.[18] As such, according to these legal scholars, Christianity forms the 'deep constitution' of the Union.[19] What makes a person 'Christian', in this new paradigm, is not so much spirituality, belief and prayer, but the deep-seated and generationally transmitted civilization, way of life and values. This point is best expressed in the words of one of my interviewees, Heinrich August Winkler, professor of European history at Humboldt University, Berlin:

---

[16]A. Merkel, 'EU praises Europe's Christian roots, agreeing with Pope', *Catholic News Agency (CAN)*, 28 March 2007. Available online at <http://www.catholic.org/international/international_story.php? id = 23565>.

[17]A. Merkel, 'Merkel wants EU Charter to make reference to Christianity', *Deutsche Welle News Agency*, 21 January 2007. Available online at <http://www.dw-world.de/dw/article/0,2144,2320266,00.html>.

[18]A. J. Menéndez, 'A Christian or a Laïc Europe? Christian values and European identity', *Ratio Juris*, 18(2), June 2005, pp. 179–205, 183–184.

[19]Menéndez, 2005, op. cit., p. 188.

What are the Western values? The most important is separation of powers, which started to occur in the 18th century. The historical roots of the modern separation of powers goes back to the separation of powers between the church and the state in European Christendom. Western values are linked to Christianity, but not absolutely.... In principle, a non-Western and non-Christian country like Turkey can adopt Western values, without sharing Christianity and Western history. However, this westernisation will take a very long-time and it will not be completed in ten to fifteen years. A long time is necessary.[20]

This new discourse applies a series of critical transformations to the meaning and function of Christianity. In the first place, it re-articulates Christianity as a set of completely secular values and attitudes. Secondly, it affirms those values as being the constituent elements of European identity. Thirdly, by assuming that those values can be acquired by a community only in the *long durée* of history and by way of generational transmission, it ascribes a 'genetic' characteristic to European identity, thereby making Europeanness an identity that one cannot acquire but has to be born into. Fourthly, it assumes that Muslims and other people who do not come from a Christian tradition, and who do not share the 'genetic pool' of Europeanness, would therefore have a hard time in acquiring European values and getting 'integrated' into European societies. Fifthly, by so doing, the right-wing political discourse transforms the metaphysical problem of religion into a this-worldly problem, by articulating it in the well-known language of 'integration'. This new paradigm makes conversion a virtual impossibility. Conversion to Christianity as religion in no way guarantees conversion to Christianity as civilization, to be understood here as a set of historically transmitted secular values and identity markers. Hence, even if a non-Western person, such as a Turk in Germany or an Algerian in France, chooses to convert to Christianity, he or she cannot become a 'civilizational Christian' and thus a 'true European', because he or she does not carry the Christian 'heritage' in his or her 'cultural genes'.

How does Turkey fit into this European right-wing discourse on religion? The argument can be put in a nutshell as follows: We cannot integrate Muslim Turkey into the ('civilizationally Christian') EU, because we could not integrate Muslim immigrants into the ('civilizationally C\hristian') French, German and other European societies. Sylvie Goulard, a French intellectual and an ardent opponent of Turkish accession to the EU, has expressed this position very clearly:

By underestimating the concrete difficulties our societies have to properly integrate Muslims already living in our communities, [if we admit Turkey into the EU] we could in the end be increasing the risk of a 'clash of civilisations' within Europe, instead of avoiding it.[21]

---

[20]Interview with Professor H. A. Winkler, Berlin, Germany, 18 October 2005.

[21]S. Goulard, 'Challenge Europe Issue 12: Europe: how wide? How deep?', *European Policy Centre*, 13 September 2004. Available online at <http://www.theepc.be/en/default. asp?TYP = CE&LV = 177&see = y&t = 42&PG = CE/EN/detail&l = 2&AI = 377>.

Nicolas Sarkozy, leader of the largest right-wing party in France, shared Goulard's view:

> We have a problem of integration of Muslims that raises the issue of Islam in Europe. To say it is not a problem is to hide from reality. If you let one hundred million Turkish Muslims come in, what will come of it?[22]

Even the long-standing secular tradition of Muslim Turkey does not make it any more 'integrateable' to Europe, because it is generally believed that Turkish secularism is fake, it is artificial, it has been assimilated by a small Westernized elite, it has not submerged into the 'cultural genes' of the larger Turkish society, and it has been protected only by the force of arms. 'The army is the only force that might stop Islamism in Turkey', say the authors of a French anti-Turkey website. 'Turkey's accession to the EU would mean that the army would have been withdrawn from the political and economic life. Hence, the accession of Turkey to the EU is likely to cause the total swing of Turkey to Islamism.'[23]

Feudal Islam, submissive women, savage men

Historically, the image of Islam and Muslims in Europe has not been particularly bright. As observed by many scholars of European identity, Islam for centuries represented the 'other' in European identity constructions. This supposed 'otherness' of Islam, in contrast to the Judeo-Christian tradition, is perhaps best captured in the following words of Max Weber:

> Islam displays other characteristics of a distinctively feudal spirit: the obviously unquestioned acceptance of slavery, serfdom, and polygamy; the disesteem for and subjection of women; the essentially ritualistic character of religious obligations; and finally, the great simplicity of religious requirements and the even greater simplicity of the modest ethical requirements.... Judaism and Christianity were specifically bourgeois-urban religions, whereas for Islam the city had only political importance.... Islam, in contrast to Judaism, lacked the requirement of a comprehensive knowledge of the law and lacked the intellectual training in casuistry which nurtured the rationalism of Judaism. The ideal personality type in the religion of Islam was not the scholarly scribe (Literat), but the warrior.... Islam was diverted completely from any really methodical control of life by the advent of the cults of saints, and finally by magic.[24]

What do European publics mean exactly when they talk about 'Islam' in particular or 'religion' in general? In a previous qualitative research that I conducted among citizens from five major EU countries (Britain, France, Italy, Germany, Spain) who stayed in Istanbul for three months or longer, I observed that the European respondents interpreted religion not so much as a theological

---

[22]N. Sarkozy, 'As election fever rises, Sarkozy consolidates his Turkey position', *Turkish Daily News*, 7 October 2006. Available online at <http://www.turkishdailynews.com.tr/article.php?enewsid = 56013>.

[23]See <http://www.nonalaturquie.com>. For a similar formulation, see the speech by UMP deputy, Philippe Pemezec, in the French Parliament, 14 October 2006.

[24]M. Weber, *Economy and Society Volume 1*, edited by Guenther Roth and Claus Wittich, University of California Press, Berkeley and Los Angeles, 1978, p. 626.

system, but as a way of life. Seventeen ordinary persons were interviewed for this research in autumn 2002. Nine were men and eight women, with an average age of 37. The main reason for most of them to come and live in Istanbul was business, followed by marriage and educational exchange. What the respondents were opposed to in Islam was not its theological system but the way of life they believed it breeds. As far as religion was concerned, for the modern Europeans, in contrast to their medieval counterparts, what really mattered was not so much differences in the ways people understood and prayed for God. They were not opposed to Islam as a belief system and did not necessarily consider Muslims as infidels and unbelievers. Actually, they did not appear to know or care much about the theological aspects of religion, whether Christianity or Islam. What they were most sensitive about were the ways in which religion shaped and influenced people's social and political lives. In that sense, almost all European respondents said that religion was important but that it must stay in its proper place, which is the personal sphere, and must not be allowed to play a role in politics, law and society. They said they were opposed to Islam so long as it is mobilized as a social, political and cultural force to deny the rights of women and to drive people away from a modern life.[25]

These observations are supported by the findings of two recent Europe-wide opinion polls. In a survey conducted in the spring of 2006 in nine EU member countries (UK, France, Germany, Netherlands, Italy, Poland, Portugal, Slovakia, Spain), Turkey and the USA, it was found that 91 per cent of the respondents in the EU countries surveyed believe that radical Islam poses an important threat to Europe. The figure is 91 per cent in France and 95 per cent in Germany. In a similar vein, according to the findings of the Transatlantic Trends' 2006 survey mentioned above, 88 per cent of the sample in the nine EU member countries surveyed believe that the values of Islam are not compatible with the values of democracy. The figure is 95 per cent in France and 98 per cent in Germany.[26] Another survey, conducted by the Pew Research Centre in 2006, found that the overwhelming majority of the publics in the largest EU member countries expressed the opinion that Muslims are not respectful of women. The figure was 80 per cent for Germany and 77 per cent for France.[27]

This brings us to the issue of gender inequality in Islam. Islamic gender relations, for almost all European respondents, are centred upon the subordination of women to men, and the headscarf is the very symbol of that subordination, which is often referred to as 'gender apartheid' by Western writers.[28] In other words, the headscarf and what it is believed to epitomize— women's enslavement—is taken to be the very antithesis, the reversal, of European modernity. The latter has evolved, as the narrative of modernization has it, along with the liberation of women and the equalization of gender

---

[25]H. Yilmaz, 'European narratives on everyday Turkey: interviews with Europeans living in Turkey', in H. Yilmaz (ed.), *Placing Turkey on the Map of Europe*, Bogazici University Press, Istanbul, 2005, pp. 23–42.

[26]Transatlantic Trends, 2006, op. cit.

[27]Pew Research Centre, Pew Global Attitudes Project, Spring 2006 Survey: Europe's Muslims More Moderate: The Great Divide: How Westerners and Muslims View Each Other, 15 nation survey conducted in spring 2006 and released on 22 June 2006. Available online at <www.pewglobal.org>.

[28]For a discussion of the terms 'gender apartheid' or 'Islamic apartheid' see <http://en.wikipedia.org/wiki/Criticism_of_Islam#_note-82>.

relations. The idea that a woman could be both Muslim and modern, wear a headscarf and at the same time become free of male domination, seems not to have gained much currency beyond academic circles. Hence, many educated women vehemently oppose the headscarf out of the conviction that any tolerance for it today would strengthen the hands of not only Muslim but also Christian and other conservatives, leading sooner or later to a deterioration of women's hard-won rights on the European plane.[29]

A closer reading of the texts on this issue reveals that the headscarf, and what it is believed to stand for, namely, women's submission to men, has a deeper meaning, corresponding to the European understanding of the difference between civilization and barbarism. To put it in a nutshell, civilization connotes a process of the socialization of male biological instincts and their re-direction from destructive to constructive ends. Barbarism represents a culture dominated by an uncontrolled, un-socialized and ultimately destructive male psyche. The liberation of women and the equalization of the male and female genders in both the public and private spheres constitutes the very essence of modern European civilization, by creating a series of institutional and normative constraints on male energy and thereby re-channelling it to peaceful, creative and productive goals. Reviewing a number of best-selling popular texts on Islam recently published in Western Europe and North America, Sherene Razack notes that:

> the violence Muslim women endure at the hands of Muslim men becomes a marker of Muslim men's barbarism … As fatally pre-modern, tribal, non-democratic and religious, the barbarism of Islam is principally evident in the treatment of women in Muslim communities. … saving Muslim women from the excesses of their society marks both Western men and Western women as more civilised.[30]

If forced marriage, forced pregnancy, beating and honour crimes constitute the basic forms of violence that Muslim men direct against Muslim women, rape is said to be the most common form of violence of Muslim men against Western women. Jamie Glazov, the Russian-born Canadian historian and managing editor of the right-wing online *Frontpage Magazine*, in an article called 'Muslim Rape, Feminist Silence', quotes two Muslim clergymen, one in Australia and the other one in Denmark, who normalized the rape of Australian and Danish women by Muslim immigrants by saying that 'unveiled women who get raped deserve it' and that 'women who do not veil themselves, and allow themselves to be "uncovered meat", are at fault if they are raped'. The clergymen's judgments, according to Glazov, are 'legitimised by various Islamic texts and numerous social and legal Islamic structures'.[31]

While rape represents the basic form of sexual violence, terror is certainly the most important type of political violence associated with Muslim men. Hence,

---

[29]K. S. Hymowitz, 'Why feminism is AWOL on Islam', *City Journal*, Winter 2003. Available online at <http://www.city-journal.org/html/issue_13_1.html>.

[30]S. H. Razack, 'Geopolitics, culture clash and gender after 9/11', paper presented at Challenge, Change & Cha Cha Cha: A Conference on Women, Feminism and the Law, organized by Women's Legal Service, Brisbane, Canada, October 2004, pp. 3–4. Available online at <http://www.wlsq.org.au/sub%20webs/conference%20pages/CCC%20Conf/CCC%20Conf%20papers.htm>.

[31]J. Glazov, 'Muslim rape, feminist silence', *FrontPageMagazine.com*, 1 November 2006. Available online at <http://www.frontpagemag.com/Articles/ReadArticle.asp?ID = 25226>.

Table 1. Types and targets of 'unchained' male violence in Islam

	Against Muslim women	Against Western women
Sexual violence	Forced marriage Forced pregnancy Banning from public life Polygamy Beating Honour crimes	Rape, sexual harassment
	Against Muslim peoples	Against Western peoples
Political violence	Authoritarian repression, human rights violations, torture	Terror, suicide bombings

according to the so-called 'terrorist profiling' policies, which gained wide currency in North America and Western Europe following the events of 9/11, the mere fact of being an Arab- or Muslim-looking young male was taken to be a sufficient reason to suspect a person as a potential terrorist. Friso Roscam Abbing, spokesman of EU Home Affairs and Justice Commissioner Franco Frattini, claimed that 'positive profiling' of potential terrorists 'would ensure that "trusted travellers" ... could benefit from smooth airport security checks'. Those who are most likely to breach the trusted travellers' contract are, as expected, Muslim travellers, foreign or immigrant. Hence, he explained, the EU foreign ministers had agreed to examine 'whether it is possible and politically desirable ... to institute a Europe-wide training program for imams to make sure their preaching is in line with EU and member-state laws'.[32] Table 1 summarizes the major types and targets of the destructive male energy of Muslim men.

For modern Europeans, fascism, in both its pre- and post-Second World War manifestations, with its exaltation of unconstrained masculinity on secular or religious grounds, its jubilation of 'Teutonic' or other pre-modern values over the modern ones, and its attempt to demolish all civic ideologies and institutions that have been built to administer male energy, embodies the archetypal European form of pure barbarism. Seen from this perspective, the wearing of the headscarf, symbolizing the subordination of women to men within the Islamic communities in Europe, including Turkey itself, means for many Europeans an uncontrolled release of dangerous male energy from the civilizing impact of women, a return to the dark ages, a breakdown of Western civilization, a resurgence of barbarism and, finally, a resurrection of fascism. Hence, it is no coincidence that terms like 'Islamic fascism' or 'Islamofascism' have been gaining wide currency among the American and European media, politicians and public intellectuals, to designate repressive Islamic fundamentalist movements inclined towards terrorism. Nick Cohen, a noted British journalist, author and political commentator, in an article published in *The Observer* accused the left of being apologists of Islamofascism: 'Islamic fascism is still fascism ... Islamofascism has been ripping through the Arab world ... and it should be the Left's worst nightmare. It's everything the

---

[32]A. Lobjakas, 'EU: terrorist threat puts "profiling" on agenda', *RFE/RL*, 18 August 2006. Available online at <http://www.rferl.org/featuresarticle/2006/08/4ad3a4df-f738-4d74-a1f0-3016cee87548.html>.

Left has resisted since the French revolution.'[33] Islamic revival touches upon many, thorough-going and deep-seated strings in the modern European psyche, and it signifies much more than a simple question of inter-cultural dialogue, alliance of civilizations and multiculturalism. Ironically, scared by the potential fascism they see embodied in the Islamic resurgence among immigrant Muslim communities, many Europeans in countries like France, Germany, the Netherlands and Austria, have taken refuge in their own fascist movements. This fear of Muslim 'barbarism' and the resulting flood towards European 'barbarism' has been massively accelerated by September 11, by the Madrid and London bombings, the killing of the Dutch filmmaker, Theo Van Gogh, and the riots and car-burnings in the Muslim-populated suburbs of Paris.

Concluding remarks

In both France and Germany, historical memory, as narrated and codified in school books for example, typically treats Turkey as falling outside the physical and cultural boundaries of Europe. Current popular images of Turkey, shaped largely by day-to-day encounters between ordinary French and German citizens and Turkish or Muslim immigrants living in those countries, have reinforced the claims of this codified historical memory that Turkey does not belong to Europe. How do identity considerations influence political choices? First of all, they do so to the extent that political leaders take account of public opinion when making domestic or foreign policy decisions. Hence, when French and German public opinion turned against Turkey's membership in the EU, as they did in recent years, it becomes very difficult for political leaders to come forward in defence of Turkey, even if they believe that, on the grounds of pure rational interest calculations, Turkish accession to the EU makes sense. This was the difficult position that the former French President, Jacques Chirac, often found himself in. Sometimes, the negative public stance against Turkey was used by certain political leaders as a bullet to kill another proposal that they opposed, by establishing a link, in the public discourse, between that proposal and the Turkish issue. That happened with the EU Constitution in France. Those opposed to the Constitution tied it to the issue of Turkish EU membership, arguing that saying yes in the constitutional referendum meant saying yes to Turkish accession. In this way, they managed to divert part of the general antipathy for Turkey to the EU Constitution, and this became yet another factor behind the French 'non' in the May 2005 referendum.

In some cases, political leaders themselves may hold strong personal opinions regarding identity, without necessarily responding to the waves coming from below. This appears to be the case with both Nicolas Sarkozy and Angela Merkel. Both leaders have made clear their desire for a tightly united, federal EU, which French politicians have termed as '*Europe puissance*'. This federal EU would be a global power centre, in the economic, political and military sense, on a par with the existing and newly emerging global powers such as the USA, Russia, Japan, China and India. Building this powerful EU, according to the leaders of the French and German right, requires a relatively homogeneous European population, in terms of shared historical legacies and common cultural values.

---

[33]See N. Cohen's remarks at <http://en.wikipedia.org/wiki/Islamofascism#_note-wh>.

The assumption that a powerful state, in this case a federal EU, can only be built upon a culturally homogeneous nation, is a peculiarly French and German idea, originating in the specific nation-building experiences of these two countries. Sarkozy and Merkel are committed to keeping Turkey outside the EU, precisely because they believe that its inclusion would permanently disrupt the cultural harmony among the European populations, bringing an end to all their attempts to build a united and strong 'European state'. In the case of Sarkozy and Merkel, historical memory, identity considerations and rational interest calculations seem to have been mingled together in a particular mix.

How can these anti-Turkish identity narratives be countered? According to a well-known study on 'national brands', the historically formed and deeply ingrained 'brand image' of a nation—for instance, the widespread geographic, historical and religious convictions in Europe regarding Turkey—changes only very slowly and over a long period of time.[34] This means that there is not much that can be done, at least in the short term, to change the historically formed images which exclude Turkey from Europe. In the short and medium term, say in the span of 5–10 years, perhaps the best way to improve Turkey's image in Europe is to try to appeal to the other self-conception of Europe, which is based on what can be called the 'Enlightenment values', encompassing universalism, humanism, rationalism, tolerance, individual rights and democracy. This other self-definition of Europe, stemming from the secular values of the Enlightenment, is equally, if not more, powerful, compared to the European values built upon the ideas of geography, history and religion. One empirical indicator of the predominance of Enlightenment values in shaping European self-perceptions can be found in the 2001 cross-country qualitative study on European identity, referred to above. In this study, when talking about what they believed constituted the fundamental European values, respondents mentioned the terms 'religion' and 'Christianity' only five times; on the other hand, they made 83 references to 'democracy' and 'human rights'.[35] 'Enlightenment values' also form the core values of the EU, as embodied for instance in the Copenhagen criteria. Turkish Muslims cannot change their religion, but the Turkish government can certainly improve the rights and status of Turkish women, whose liberties are curtailed in the larger society partly with a reference to Islamic beliefs and traditions. The Turkish state cannot be relocated to central Europe, but it can certainly do more to increase dialogue and cooperation with other European countries at the level of civil society. Finally, many more steps can be taken to improve the Turkish record on human rights. Taking the right steps in the direction of 'Enlightenment values' appears to be the best option for making a meaningful positive change in Turkey's image in Europe in the short term.

---

[34]The Anholt Nation Brands Index, *How has our world view changed since 2005?*, Q4, 2006. Available online at <www.gmi-mr.com>.

[35]OPTEM, 2001, op. cit.

The dynamics of EU accession: Turkish travails in comparative perspective

SUSANNAH VERNEY

Enlargement on the frontiers of Europe

For several years, an air of crisis has been hanging over European integration. Ambitious plans for political deepening have run into trouble while monetary cooperation has not opened the way to political union. The European institutional structures are under strain after the recent Enlargement. The latter added some difficult new partners, not all committed to the cause of integration. Meanwhile, steps towards a common foreign policy have yet to significantly enhance Europe's global weight. Economic pressures, encouraging calls for national protectionism, seem to be undermining popular support for the fundamental bargain at the heart of integration—the opening of borders. And as if all of this is not enough, the European club is faced with the candidacy of an economically weak applicant with an unstable political past, located on the geographical periphery of Europe. One may well ask, given these circumstances, how was it possible for Greece to enter the European Community?[1]

In the first decade of the 21st century, with a heated debate raging over Turkish accession and the future of Europe, the situation outlined above may sound distinctly familiar. But in actual fact, the climate described is that of a period 30 years in the past, when the Enlargement which was proving so difficult to digest was not the Fifth but the First. In the mid-1970s, all the member states' economies were in recession following the 1973 oil price rise. The latter had also triggered the collapse of the Snake, the EC's first attempt at monetary cooperation. With economic malaise weakening support for deeper integration, the aim of achieving European Union by the end of the decade, optimistically proclaimed at the Paris summit of 1972 and examined in the Tindemans Report, was quietly dropped. Meanwhile, in launching European Political Cooperation (EPC) in 1973, the EC had taken its first steps towards a common external identity. But the unanimity requirement encouraged agreement at the level of the lowest common denominator. When the EC managed to speak with one voice, during the summer 1974 Cyprus crisis, no-one appeared to be listening.

The Greek accession application of June 1975 was thus submitted in an atmosphere of crisis, when the future of the integration process itself was presented as being under threat. In January 1976, the *Report on European Union*,

---

[1]In this paper, reference will be made to the European Community (EC) in the period preceding the ratification of the Treaty of Maastricht in 1992 and to the European Union (EU) afterwards. The acronym EC/EU will be used when referring to the experience of European integration across time.

drafted by the Belgian Prime Minister, Leo Tindemans, described 'the incompleted European structure' as 'swaying' and warned that 'the crisis in Europe is so serious that we must, in the immediate future, save what has already been achieved and, ... take drastic measures to make a significant leap forward'.[2] The parallels with the climate following the failure of the 2005 referenda on the European Constitutional Treaty are obvious.

Although the term 'Enlargement fatigue' was not to be coined for another three decades, the phenomenon it describes was already on the EC agenda. The 1973 Enlargement had increased the number of members by 50 per cent, a proportional increase unparalleled in any subsequent Enlargement. The UK was proving particularly hard to digest, having already demanded a renegotiation of its entry terms and promoting a quite different vision of integration from the EC's founder members. Absorption capacity, although also an unknown term, was also very much an issue. In February 1976, when the decision was announced to open accession negotiations with Greece, the first question asked by the press concerned the compatibility of this new Enlargement with the deepening and strengthening of the Community.[3] Just a few days earlier, the Brussels-based daily *Agence Europe* had asked, 'up to what size can the Community function in satisfactory conditions according to the present procedures?' Reflecting another preoccupation which appears very contemporary today, the same article also raised the question of the frontiers of Europe, asking whether the Community should set geographical limits to its expansion.[4]

Thus, what is striking is the extent to which the prospect of Greek accession in the mid-1970s raised issues and themes which clearly resonate today. This paper aims to pursue the comparison further, to see whether the Greek experience can illuminate Turkey's 'long and possibly winding'[5] road to accession. This may seem an unusual comparison to make. The Turkish accession process is more often compared with that of the Central and Eastern European countries (CEECs) which entered the European Union in 2004.[6] The premise of this paper, however, is that the dynamics of accession display some important constants which make the Greek experience potentially relevant to its would-be partner.

A special case?

To date, negotiations for entry to the EC/EU have always concluded successfully.[7] This universal experience has resulted in the negotiating process

---

[2]Commission of the European Communities, European Union: Report by Mr Leo Tindemans to the European Council, *Bulletin of the European Communities*, Supplement 1/76, pp. 7, 11.

[3]S. Haritos, *Ellada-EOK, 1959–1979: Apo ti Syndesi stin Entaxi*, Papazissis, Athens, p. 201.

[4]*Agence Europe*, 22 January 1976.

[5]As described by Enlargement Commissioner, Olli Rehn, in *The Guardian*, 30 June 2005.

[6]And especially the Polish case. E.g. see A. Schrijvers, 'What can Turkey learn from previous accession negotiations?', in E. LaGro and K. E. Jørgensen (eds), *Turkey and the European Union: Prospects for a Difficult Encounter*, Palgrave Macmillan, Basingstoke and New York, 2007, pp. 29–50; A. Lundgren, 'The limits of Enlargement', in H. Sjursen (ed.), *Enlargement and the Finality of the EU*, Arena, Oslo, 2002, pp. 35–48.

[7]As is well known, the only country which negotiated accession but did not subsequently enter the EC/EU was Norway—twice—but this was due on both occasions to the rejection of EU membership by the Norwegian people in referendums and not to a breakdown in negotiations.

acquiring the image of a 'ritual dance', moving towards a preordained positive conclusion. This picture of inevitability appears to be challenged by the Turkish case, which, in the words of Loukas Tsoukalis, forms 'a category of its own'.[8] The distinctiveness of the Turkish candidacy has been summed up by the same author in three words: 'big, poor and different'. With a population of 71.6 million inhabitants in 2005, Turkey would become the second largest EU state and in terms of institutional weight, the second most powerful member.[9] Its EU entry would upset the existing balance among the member states, challenging the pre-eminence of the Big Three and displacing France from its position as the EU's second largest member. Turkey's size, in combination with its low GDP per capita—only 27 per cent of the average for the EU-25 in 2005—makes economic integration a major challenge, necessitating sweeping reforms if EU policies are to be sustainable. Moreover, as Europe's historical 'Other',[10] a predominantly Muslim society and a state without a history of strong commitment to democratic processes, Turkey has often been viewed as an alien body which does not belong within the European community. Finally, to compound its problems, Turkey faces a special obstacle in the form of the Cyprus issue.

Due to all these factors, the Turkish candidacy has evoked unprecedented opposition, both from public opinion and political elites. As a result, it took Turkey over 12 years from its March 1987 accession application to the achievement of formal candidate status at the Helsinki summit in December 1999. A further six years elapsed before the official opening of entry negotiations in October 2005. In 2004, when the EU was due to decide whether to give Turkey a date for the opening of accession negotiations, open opponents included European Commissioner, Fritz Bolkestein, European Convention Chairman, Valéry Giscard d'Estaing, and German opposition leader, Angela Merkel. A year later, the opening of negotiations was openly opposed by the Austrian government, which only backed down at the last minute. Following the election of French President Sarkozy in May 2007, for the first time ever an ongoing accession negotiation has been publicly opposed by the head of an EU member state—and moreover, by one of its most powerful members. In this climate, the negotiations have made little progress. The best case scenarios were initially for the Turkish entry talks to last 10–15 years. But 20 months after they began, only three negotiating chapters had been opened and only one closed.

Enlargement to Turkey therefore remains an enigma. Will the Turkish application follow the tested path of ultimately successful accession negotiations, albeit in a more protracted version than any previous case? Or will it turn out to be the exception that proves the rule? In the belief that current Turkish travails can be better understood in comparative perspective, this paper will examine the successful Greek negotiation, first focusing on the problems which Greece

---

[8]Tsoukalis, 'The JCMS Lecture: Managing diversity and change in the European Union', *Journal of Common Market Studies*, 44(1), pp. 1–15. Diverging from this view of exceptionalism is Kirsty Hughes, who suggests that 'Turkey will have significant impacts on the Union but these impacts can be managed as those of previous Enlargements have been'. K. Hughes, 'Turkey and the European Union: just another Enlargement?', Friends of Europe Working Paper, Brussels, 2004.

[9]R. Baldwin and M. Widgren, 'The impact of Turkey's membership on voting in the EU', Centre for European Policy Studies, Brussels, Policy Brief No. 62, 2005.

[10]E.g. I. B. Neumann, *Uses of the Other: 'The East' in European Identity Formation*, University of Minnesota Press, Minneapolis, 1999.

encountered and then assessing the strategy which it pursued to overcome them. It will conclude by examining the implications of the Greek experience for Turkey's accession process.

A difficult start

Greece was formally recognized as a candidate for EC membership in February 1976, just eight months after submitting its application for EC membership. Negotiations opened in July 1976 and were concluded in April 1979, followed by accession on 1 January 1981. Hence, the whole process took just five and a half years from start to finish. Thus, from a Turkish perspective, Greece appears to have had an easy accession. However, this was not the way it looked to the Greeks. The latter had only one previous case of accession negotiations with which to compare their own treatment. They regarded the First Enlargement as setting a series of precedents which should be followed in the Greek case. When this did not happen, the Greeks, like the Turks subsequently, felt they were being treated in a discriminatory fashion in comparison with their predecessors.

The Greek government formally announced its intention of applying for full EC membership in September 1974, just two months after the fall of the military dictatorship which had ruled the country since 1967. Some of the contemporary newspaper coverage suggests that the decision to open negotiations with Greece was taken with some reluctance. In the months preceding the official membership bid, *The Economist* referred to the Community as welcoming Greece with 'half-open arms' and claimed that 'the way Greece is forcing the pace is acutely embarrassing for the Nine'. Following the submission of the accession application, the same publication described the attitude of the Nine as 'guarded' and declared that several EEC countries were 'speaking with forked tongues ... approving in public but not in private'.[11] It seems possible that *The Economist*'s coverage may have reflected concerns which the British government preferred not to express openly.

These reservations were reflected in the European Commission's *Opinion* on the Greek application, published on 29 January 1976. In contrast to its negative response to Turkey in 1989, the Commission declared that the Community should give Greece a 'clear positive answer'. However, as I. Tsalicoglou has remarked, 'the quality of its affirmation left a lot to be desired'.[12] Instead of the immediate opening of negotiations, the Commission proposed an innovation not to be found in the Treaty of Rome: a 'pre-accession' period of unspecified duration, during which the Community would provide financial assistance to enable Greece to carry out necessary structural reforms. Tsoukalis refers to 'rumours' that this proposal was the work of the Commission's British Vice-President, Sir Christopher Soames. He comments that 'if this was so, it is difficult to imagine that such an initiative did not have the backing of the British government'.[13]

---

[11]*The Economist*, 7 December 1974, 10 May 1975, 26 July 1975, 21 August 1975.

[12]I. Tsalicoglou, *Negotiating for Entry: The Accession of Greece to the European Community*, Dartmouth, Aldershot, 1995, p. 30.

[13]L. Tsoukalis, *The European Community and its Mediterranean Enlargement*, George Allen & Unwin, London, 1980, p. 135.

Within Greece, the 'pre-accession' period evoked uproar, being widely interpreted as an attempt to delay Greek accession indefinitely.[14] Adding fuel to the fire, it was felt that additional conditions had been raised in the Greek case which previous candidates had not been asked to meet. These conditions were particularly controversial because they were political. The call for Greece and Turkey to find 'a just and lasting solution' to their differences provoked a furious reaction in Greece, where it was felt that the Commission was venturing into fields outside its areas of competence. While the *Opinion* also stated that it would be 'inappropriate for the decision on Greek membership to be dependent' on the solution of the Greek–Turkish dispute,[15] the fact the issue had been raised at all resulted in even pro-EC Greek politicians claiming that Turkey was being given a veto over Greek accession.[16]

The publication of the *Opinion* was followed by 13 days of 'unprecedented tension' in Greek–EC relations.[17] Dynamic diplomacy on the part of the Greek government, combined with intra-institutional divisions and inter-institutional rivalries within the EC, determined the outcome. The Commission itself was divided over the Greek 'Opinion', with only seven of the 13 Commissioners voting in favour of the pre-accession period. Several EC member governments also reacted unfavourably to what was seen as a Commission attempt to usurp the responsibilities of the Council of Ministers. According to Tsoukalis, at the crucial Council meeting which decided to open negotiations, 'the lack of enthusiasm for Greece's entry was compensated for by the simple fact that no member government wanted to be seen opposing it'.[18] 'After a long discussion in very restricted session', the Greek accession application was formally accepted and it was agreed to open negotiations 'as soon as possible'.[19]

Good neighbourliness

Although 'pre-accession' had been rejected, linkage between Greek EC entry, EC–Turkey relations and by extension, the Greek–Turkish dispute, had been clearly established. The next hurdle for the Greek side was the formal opening of accession negotiations, which the Community explicitly made dependent on a prior or simultaneous meeting of the Turkish–EC Association Council.[20] The negative response of the Turkish government to this initiative affected the timing of the official opening ceremony, resulting in several weeks delay. Then, in what was widely interpreted as an attempt to prevent the start of the negotiations, on 10 July the Turkish government sent a ship to survey the seabed in a contested area of the Aegean. The Greek government responded to the ensuing Aegean crisis with restraint, with the result that negotiations formally opened on 27 July.

---

[14]See the Greek press for 30 and 31 January 1976.

[15]Commission of the European Communities, op. cit., p. 8.

[16]See *Agence Europe*, 31 January 1976.

[17]J. Siotis, 'The politics of Greek accession', Sussex European Papers: The Mediterranean Challenge VI, University of Sussex, 1981, p. 102.

[18]Tsoukalis, *Mediterranean Enlargement*, op. cit., p. 136.

[19]*Agence Europe*, 10 February 1976.

[20]*Agence Europe*, 1 and 9 July 1976.

Although the 'good neighbourliness' criterion was not part of the formal agenda of Greece's entry talks, it was a key issue at the second and even more crucial level of negotiations—the constant high level political contacts which formed the essential framework within which the technical talks developed. Reassuring Greece's partners that its accession would not embroil the Community in the Greek–Turkish dispute became a fundamental element of the Greek negotiating process. The Greek government not only made an explicit commitment not to block Turkey's aspirations to EC membership,[21] but was always careful to reassure its future partners that Greek EC entry would not raise the tension in the Eastern Mediterranean. At a particularly crucial point in the entry negotiations, for example, the Greek Prime Minister met with his Turkish counterpart, resulting in a joint statement confirming 'the political will of their governments to seek peaceful and just solutions to the[ir] problems'.[22] The Greek government also went out of its way to show sympathy for Turkish problems, for example, by expressing its understanding for the reasons for the 1980 coup[23] and making symbolic gestures such as its abstention during a UN vote on the Armenian genocide.[24]

From one crisis to the next

Meanwhile, it was generally accepted that the Greek negotiations were 'slow moving'.[25] The negotiations for the First Enlargement had been completed in 18 months (June 1970–January 1972). The fact the Greek negotiations dragged on for 34 months was interpreted in the Greek press as discriminatory treatment and even as a way of fulfilling the Commission's aim of a 'pre-accession' period through the back door. The negotiations were not only slow. They were also accompanied by high political drama.

The first of a series of crises occurred in January 1977, when the leaders of the Greek negotiating team resigned in protest at what was seen as the Community's hard-line stance. Greece initially hoped that, for reasons of equity, just as the Greek government had accepted the *acquis communautaire* as the basis for the negotiations, the EC would reciprocate by recognizing the rights which Greece had acquired under its 1961 Association Agreement. However, the Community insisted from the start that this prior relationship was not relevant to the accession talks, which had created 'a new situation'. This aroused considerable resentment in Greece and divided the pro-accession camp, with the pro-European opposition parties calling for the government to take a tough line. The issue was resolved by a Greek capitulation on the *acquis d'Association* and the replacement of the national negotiating team.

---

[21]R. Clogg, 'Troubled alliance: Greece and Turkey', in R. Clogg (ed.), *Greece in the 1980s*, Macmillan, London and Basingstoke, 1983, p. 141.

[22]For a detailed account of the Montreux meeting, see K. Svolopoulos, *Konstantinos Karamanlis: Archeio, Gegonota & Keimena*, Vol. 10, Idryma Konstantinos G. Karamanlis/Ekdotiki Athinon, Athens, pp. 133–144.

[23]Clogg, op. cit., p. 141.

[24]See *Kathimerini*, 20 March 1979.

[25]*The Times*, 1 February 1977.

After the *acquis* crisis came the 'globalization' drama. When the Greek application was submitted in June 1975, Iberian accession appeared a distant prospect. Spain was still ruled by Franco while a year after the overthrow of its dictatorship, Portugal remained in a state of revolutionary ferment. This picture changed with unanticipated rapidity. Even before Portugal and Spain submitted their accession applications in March and June 1977, it was already clear that the next Enlargement would entail the importation of a whole tier of less prosperous members, whose entry was likely to change the nature of European integration. While the admission of Greece, with its 9 million inhabitants, could have been accommodated with only marginal adjustments to the Community structures, this did not apply to Spain, the EC's future fifth largest member state. The Mediterranean Enlargement therefore magnified the dilemmas concerning EC absorption capacity.

For the Community, a logical approach appeared to be the 'globalization' of negotiations, entailing simultaneous entry talks with all three South European applicants so the problems of the new Enlargement could be confronted as a whole. Almost overnight, Greek accession turned into a most uncertain prospect. In the best case scenario, 'globalization' would have led to major delays, both for substantive reasons concerning the greater complexity of the Spanish case and for procedural ones, as the Iberian states were so far behind in the accession process. The Greek government responded with a round of intensive diplomatic activity throughout the spring of 1977, repeatedly seeking assurances that its application would be treated 'on its own merits', separately from any other candidacy. Although the immediate danger of 'globalization' was ultimately averted, there had been a complete change in the context in which Greek accession was being negotiated.

Negotiating in the Iberian shadow

Once it was viewed as the vanguard of a wider Mediterranean Enlargement, the Greek application faced unprecedented opposition from powerful national interest groups within the member states. The German trade unions were against South European workers gaining free movement of labour. Meanwhile, in spring 1977, the French farming federations adopted a public position against Enlargement in general and Greek accession specifically. Immediately, all the major French opposition parties—the Gaullists under Jacques Chirac, the socialists led by François Mitterand and the eurosceptic communist party— declared their opposition to Greek accession unless it was preceded by reform of the Common Agricultural Policy (CAP) in favour of Mediterranean agriculture.[26] This position was rapidly echoed by members of the Italian government.[27]

This sparked the third major crisis of the Greek accession negotiations. France, which under President Giscard d'Estaing had previously been one of the chief 'drivers' of Greek accession, suddenly became the leading 'brakeman'. Under pre-election pressure, with municipal elections due in the autumn of 1977

---

[26]G. Kontogeorgis, *I Ellada stin Evropi: I Poreia Pros tin Enosi kai i Politiki Karamanli*, Christos Giovanis, Athens, 1985, pp. 95–97.

[27]*Acropolis*, 29 April 1977; *Eleftherotypia*, 20 June 1977.

and parliamentary polls in the spring of 1978, Giscard's government shifted its stance. From June 1977, it began to demand that reform of the CAP take place in parallel with the Enlargement negotiations. As subsequent experience has repeatedly proved, CAP reform is one of the most contentious issues on the European integration agenda. In the 1970s, the French and Italian goal of improving the regimes for Mediterranean products entailed increasing CAP spending at a time when the UK was seeking drastic cuts. The Greek accession negotiations were thus in danger of becoming embroiled in the British budget dispute. The latter was already causing considerable intra-Community acrimony and after the election of Mrs Thatcher in 1979, was to bring the EC to the verge of paralysis. Thus, like 'globalization', the issue of parallel CAP reform could only appear as yet another attempt to postpone Greek accession indefinitely.

It was not until the French parliamentary elections of April 1978 were safely over, with a victory for Giscard d'Estaing's party, that the French government dropped the demand for parallel CAP reform. One can only speculate on the consequences for the Greek accession negotiations if the French opposition had won the elections. The new government would undoubtedly have acted as a serious constraint on President Giscard's Enlargement policy. It seems improbable that the Greek accession negotiations would have been completed just one year later.

But with the French problem resolved, in July 1978 the negotiations finally entered their substantive phase. As P. K. Ioakeimidis notes, for 17 months no real progress had been made, as 'the Community had avoided giving its own negotiating positions' and was 'particularly unwilling' to reveal its hand on the two most vital questions: transitional periods and agriculture.[28] From the start of the talks, the Greeks, following the precedent of the First Enlargement, had demanded a maximum transitional period of five years across all sectors. Instead, in the sensitive field of free movement of labour, the Community made an unprecedented demand for a 15-year transitional period. To add insult to injury, free movement was a right which Greece should have acquired after 1974 under the terms of its Association Agreement. However, after the fall of the Greek dictatorship, the EC had simply refused to open negotiations on the subject. Meanwhile, with regard to agriculture, the Greeks had proposed that transitional periods should only apply to sensitive Community products entering the Greek market, rather than the other way about.[29] In autumn 1978, one of the major bones of contention became the Community insistence on the opposite principle, that is, on using transitional periods—longer than those demanded in the First Enlargement—to protect the markets of the richer EC members from the competition of the less prosperous new entrant.

A final negotiating crisis occurred in December 1978, when the Greek government faced budget proposals which would have led to the country subsidizing its partners. Under the original EC proposals, Greece, with a GDP per capita well below even the poorest current EC members,[30] was asked to pay

---

[28]P. K. Ioakeimidis, *He Scheseis Elladas-EOK-PA*, Papazissis, Athens, 2nd edn, 1977, p. 57.

[29]A. Ioannides, 'Negotiating for accession: pressures and constraints', MA thesis, University of Sussex, p. 47.

[30]According to the European Commission's 'Opinion', in 1973 Greek per capita GDP was 84 per cent that of Ireland and 70 per cent that of Italy.

a net contribution of 30 million ecus during its first year of membership.[31] At this point, as related by G. Kontogeorgis, the Greek minister responsible for relations with the EC, Prime Minister Karamanlis threatened to publicly denounce the Community for its harsh stance.[32] Although the Community then accepted the principle that Greece should not become a net contributor, it took another three months to sort out the details.

Thus, only in retrospect and in comparison with the even more difficult cases that came after, can Greece's accession negotiations appear to have been moving towards a preordained positive conclusion. In reality, Greece's road to accession was neither straight nor smooth, but winding and bumpy. Every stage of the negotiations was difficult, with the Community taking a considerably tougher stance than in the previous Enlargement as well as adding informal political conditions. It is clear that the whole accession process could so easily have been derailed if the Greeks had allowed it to be.

Deferring the day

Viewed in historical perspective, Enlargement appears as a fundamental element of the European integration process, its political and economic dynamism and its image as a successful enterprise. Paradoxically, however, the EC/EU has consistently appeared to embark on Enlargement with reluctance, never seeming to consider itself ready for the admission of new members.[33] In the case of the CEECs, for instance, J. I. Torreblanca describes the member states as being 'reluctantly pulled into the Enlargement process' and comments that 'the desire of the Twelve not to engage in this process was all too self-evident'.[34] So while in the Turkish case, the EU reluctance to admit new members appears in an extreme form, the reluctance itself marks a repetition of an established pattern.

However, it is easier to accept an accession application than to reject it. The costs of accepting Enlargement, including direct financial contributions and reduced institutional weight within the EU, are shared among the member states. In contrast, the costs of attempting to stop Enlargement burdens only those states prepared to appear as open opponents. For an individual government, the potential price of a veto may be considerable, both in terms of irreparable damage to relations with the rejected applicant and of the loss of credibility and goodwill among other EU members. This could entail significant penalties in a European integration process based on package deals, in which insistence on national positions in one area may require concessions in other crucial sectors.

The cost of saying 'no' has turned eventual accession into the 'default drive' outcome of a membership application. Rather than turning candidates away, the tendency has been to open negotiations, even though some governments or institutional players may be at best ambiguous about Enlargement. This is what

---

[31]See *The Scotsman*, 5 April 1979; also *The Guardian*, 5 April 1979; *The Economist*, 7 April 1979.

[32]G. Kontogeorgis, op. cit., p. 177.

[33]To date, the single exception—which may be regarded as one that proves the rule—was the Fourth Enlargement, in which the candidates concerned, all small, stable democracies, were already implementing the 'four freedoms' and would become net EU budget contributors.

[34]J. I. Torreblanca, *The Reuniting of Europe: Promises, Negotiations and Compromises*, Ashgate, Aldershot, 2001, p. 329.

happened with Greece in 1976. In 2005, despite the entrenched opposition of leading figures in the EU, the pattern was repeated in the much more difficult case of Turkey.

While the Turkish talks are the first time that some governments have been prepared to state publicly that negotiations may not end in accession, there have been previous cases in which governments seem to have secretly hoped that Enlargement would never take place. For example, in spring 1971 the UK entry talks reached impasse, due to French demands described by *The Observer* newspaper as 'an effective veto'. As Uwe Kitzinger notes, some British officials believed that:

> France, unwilling to let Britain in, and unwilling also to incur the odium of a third veto [following the two French vetoes of 1963 and 1967], was quietly tying one noose after another in which the negotiations might strangle themselves.[35]

Meanwhile, just two months before the Fifth Enlargement negotiations formally concluded, Heather Grabbe claimed that 'some EU politicians' would have been 'secretly delighted' if the whole enterprise of admitting the CEECs could have been postponed.[36]

Even when governments are potentially sympathetic, the pattern is for the agreement to negotiate to be followed by an attempt to defer the day of accession. This reflects a more general characteristic of EC/EU decision making. Ever since the drafters of the Treaty of Rome included a Common Agricultural Policy while leaving future negotiators to thrash out the details, the tendency has been to leave difficult decisions for later, when hopefully the conditions for agreement will have matured. This habit becomes particularly pronounced in the case of Enlargement, which involves a dual negotiation—first, and most difficult, among the member states themselves, and then between the member states and the candidate. There seems to have been only one occasion in the history of Enlargement when the EU took the initiative to speed up entry talks. The Fourth Enlargement was an exceptional case, with the admission of a group of prosperous established democracies seen by the EU as 'a new beacon of achievement' after the trauma of the Maastricht Treaty ratification.[37] In contrast, during the Greek talks, the preference for postponement was manifested repeatedly, with the successive proposals for 'pre-accession', 'globalization' and internal EC reform parallel to Enlargement.

While protracted negotiations may be functional for the preservation of internal balance within the EC/EU, they hold dangers for the candidate. As the Greek case illustrates, new membership applications may complicate the picture. Developments at the European level may result in delays to Enlargement while internal reform processes are completed or intra-EU crises resolved. Accession processes are also vulnerable to the electoral cycle. Elections in the member states may alter the balance of forces unfavourably for the candidate, as the French elections threatened to do with regard to Greece in 1978. Meanwhile, the

---

[35]U. Kitzinger, *Diplomacy and Persuasion: How Britain Joined the Common Market*, Thames and Hudson, London, 1973, p. 92.

[36]H. Grabbe, 'Enlargement puts EU credibility on the line: Turkey is the litmus test', *Wall Street Journal*, 11 October 2002.

[37]L. Miles, *The European Union and the Nordic Countries*, Routledge, London, 1995, pp. 69–70.

eurosceptic and anti-NATO socialist and communist parties gained over one-third of the vote. This provided a strong argument for ensuring accession took place before the next national election—if it was to happen at all. Meanwhile, Karamanlis' image as 'a man we can trust' enhanced the credibility of his country's candidacy and helped to unblock the accession negotiations at critical moments.

The third major element of the Greek onslaught on the Community citadel was a norm-based rhetorical strategy aimed at the broadest possible audience, encompassing not only the decision makers directly involved in Enlargement, but also the elite and general publics that might influence them. The official Greek discourse sought to overcome the economic and practical objections to Enlargement by presenting Greece's EC entry as a moral and political imperative. There were two basic lines of argument. The first was a continual stress on the linkage between Greek democracy and accession. On the one hand, it was claimed that Greece's democratisation after the Junta's fall entitled the country to enter the European democratic family. On the other, it was repeatedly declared that EC entry would strengthen the young Greek democracy. The second line of argument focused on the constant invocation of Greek devotion to the European ideal, manifested in its post-war Western orientation and choice to become the EC's first associate. In parallel, repeated statements of intent emphasized the Greek desire to contribute to European political unity and the deepening of political integration.

These were clever arguments, indicating an understanding that the EC did not function simply as a mechanism for promoting the interests of the member states. Instead, the Greek discourse spoke directly to the attempt to create a sense of collective identity for the European integration project as a community of values—an attempt which had gained a new momentum in the last few years before the Greek application, when the launching of EPC took the EC further into the field of political integration. In this context, both the main strands of Greek arguments underlined Greece's European identity. This identity was not substantiated only by references to the role of ancient Greek culture, although these could also be found in abundance. Instead, its basis was the proclaimed Greek attachment to the fundamental European values of democracy and European integration, with accession the right and reward of a country expressing devotion to these ideals. Meanwhile, the linkage between accession and democracy turned the former into a moral obligation for the Community member states, who were now required to prove their own commitment to these values by admitting Greece. The key point was the way in which these arguments made the admission of Greece into an issue of the Community's own credibility and consistency with its self-proclaimed identity. The effectiveness of the Greek rhetorical strategy is indicated by its subsequent imitation, first by Spain and Portugal in the Third Enlargement and then by the eight CEECs which entered the EU in 2004.

Turkey on default drive?

The Greek case study reminds us that the EC/EU habitually appears reluctant to engage in accession, which is almost always a tough process for the candidate.

As the Greek example illustrates, the first hurdle for the candidate is to get the EC/EU to the negotiating table and the second to keep up the momentum of talks once they have started. The decision to open negotiations with Greece, while not as controversial as in the Turkish case, was clearly contested. The row around the Commission's *Opinion* was brief but spectacular. Even when the negotiations started, the continued political will to admit Greece was not something which could be taken for granted. During the three and a half years of entry talks, the Greek government faced a succession of obstacles which had not originally been envisaged, as the context of the negotiations changed in response to intra-EC developments, new membership applications and the impact of national electoral cycles. In response, the EC repeatedly attempted to slow down the negotiations and delay the moment of Greek accession. The onus for ensuring the latter took place clearly lay with the candidate, whose persistence and flexible negotiating tactics finally paid off.

In the Turkish case, the usual phenomenon of EU reluctance to Enlargement is writ especially large and will be harder to overcome than previously. It is possible that in addition to continuous attempts to defer the day of accession *ad infinitum*, the Turkish application may face an open veto from one or more member states, particularly France. Turkey is not, of course, the first candidate to face a French Question. As we have seen, in 1977–1978 the united French opposition, left and right, called for a veto on Greek entry and the negotiations could not progress until the French President resolved his domestic problems. Meanwhile, in 1971 the UK entry talks remained deadlocked until the French President and British Prime Minister resolved their differences at a bilateral summit.[45] However, French opposition to Turkish entry is likely to be particularly obdurate, because the latter threatens France's leading position as the second largest member of the EU. The question, therefore, is whether the 'default drive' dynamic which makes it hard to reject Enlargement will be overturned in the difficult Turkish case.

On the French side, it is worth noting that in the initial phase after his May 2007 election, the new French President appeared to have opened simultaneous multiple fronts with his EU partners. In this context, attempting to block Turkish accession prospects might have a heavy cost for French interests. Reduced tolerance from the other EU members for French flexibility within the Stability Pact, for example, could have more immediate impact on French politics than allowing talks to continue on a Turkish accession likely to take place, if at all, under another Presidency. Past experience of accession dynamics suggests that an easier course of action for any member government opposed to Turkish membership would be to avoid a direct veto of the negotiations, but instead to follow the tested path of dragging them out as long as possible, deferring the ultimate day of decision for a future government.

On the Turkish side, it is worth remembering that for the EU to directly close the door in Turkey's face would damage the Union's own credibility. This is not only because of the promise made in 1963 that Association would lead to Turkish membership but also due to the systematic projection of European integration, since the era of the Greek accession application, as a democratisation project. Even if a national veto were to be exercised, it need not necessarily be definitive. It would always be possible to come back and try again later, as the British

---

[45]See Kitzinger, op. cit., pp. 113–125.

experience so amply demonstrates. The UK became a full EC member just six years after General de Gaulle's second veto of its application. In the case of EC/EU membership, the only irreversible act is accession itself.

While it is hard for the EU to say 'no', it would be far less of a problem if Turkey itself was to break off negotiations, thereby accepting the responsibility for their failure. Turkey does not have a good track record in this respect, having unilaterally frozen the Association Agreement in 1978. At some point, it might appear tempting for Turkey to walk away from the negotiating table again, especially given the high domestic cost of meeting EU conditionality. But as in the 1980s, this could result in the country's further relegation in the Enlargement queue.

Alternatively, the experience of the successful Greek negotiation suggests three ingredients for a corresponding Turkish strategy. The first concerns the need to remain focused on the ultimate aim of membership, making the necessary tactical concessions necessary to achieve this strategic goal. The second is the presence of a credible Turkish actor in the role of 'the man we can trust', for whose benefit sacrifices should be made by the EU and its members, while the third concerns the adoption of an effective rhetorical strategy, creating a climate conducive to Turkish accession.

With regard to the latter, the main Turkish argument to date has been that the EU should not become a Christian club. This is unlikely to be successful, not least because—as the EU's Constitutional Convention demonstrated—there is a strong current of opinion within the EU that this is precisely what the Union should be. Above all, however, this is an argument which constantly reminds the hearer that Turkey is different, rather than 'one of us'. In their examination of public opinion in the EU, A. Ruiz-Jiménez and J. I. Torreblanca noted that opposition to Turkish accession is mainly connected with identity-related arguments,[46] while R. Hilsse argues that 'what is needed for Turkey to secure membership in the EU is a discourse that emphasizes cultural similarities instead of differences'.[47] Following in the footsteps of Greece and the other 10 entrants which followed the latter's example, Turkey could claim a modern European identity on the basis of its adherence to the European values of democracy and political integration. The latter in particular has so far been more noticeable by its absence. Official Turkish discourse has done little to reassure Turkey's would-be partners that images of the country as a future Anglo-Saxon 'Trojan horse' within the EU, promoting an intergovernmental vision of European integration, do not correspond to reality.

A rhetorical strategy along these lines has become potentially more convincing since the confrontation between the civilian government and the army in spring 2007. As Ziya Önis has noted, the previous five years had already seen a reshaping of EU elite opinion in favour of Turkish membership due to the democratic reform programme pursued by the Turkish government post-2002.[48]

---

[46]A. Ruiz-Jimenez and J. I. Torreblanca, *European Public Opinion and Turkey's Accession: Making Sense of Arguments For and Against*, Working Paper No. 16, European Policy Institutes Network.

[47]R. Hilsse, 'Cool Turkey: solving the image problem to secure EU membership', *Mediterranean Politics*, 11(3), November 2006, p. 319.

[48]Z. Önis, 'Turkey's encounters with the new Europe: multiple transformations, inherent dilemmas and the challenges ahead', *Journal of Southern Europe and the Balkans*, 8(3), December 2006, pp. 279–298.

Then the April 2007 'e-coup', with which the army leadership tried to prevent the election of a President of the Republic from the governing party, suggested Turkey was in danger of democratic regression. If the challenge to the military role in Turkish politics and the pursuit of the democratic reform programme continue, this could turn support for Turkey's European prospects, as in the Greek case, into a democratic imperative for an EU which perceives itself as a community of values. Prime Minister Erdogan could then become firmly established as the Turkish 'man we can trust'. Such a development would make it particularly hard for the EU to say 'no' to Turkey.

This paper has suggested that Turkey may not be such a special case. Other examples of Enlargement, when examined in detail, prove not to have been so easy after all. By offering insight into the dynamics of the accession process, the Greek case study has also suggested ways in which Turkey could improve the odds for its accession process. Only time will tell whether this recipe will succeed and the 'default drive' dynamic will also function in the Turkish case.

Europeanisation and the transformation of Turkey's Cyprus policy: a case of democratic peace?

KIVANÇ ULUSOY and SUSANNAH VERNEY

From the beginning of the current decade, Turkey's Cyprus policy has acted as a key marker of national identity and political change, the central themes of this volume. At the same time, the Cyprus conflict as an international relations issue holds the key to future Turkey-EU relations. Its resolution will be an indispensable part of future Turkish accession to the Union. For these reasons, the case of Cyprus policy merits its own chapter of this book.

The evolution in Turkey's Cyprus policy has been a fundamental element in what Kemal Kirişci has described as Turkey's 'transformation from a "post-Cold War warrior' to an aspiring 'benign regional power"'[1]—in turn a story which has been inextricably intertwined with the country's rapprochement with the EU. During the three decades following the dramatic events of 1974, within the EU (and the EC, its pre-1993 predecessor), Turkey's continued presence in Cyprus was consistently seen as a blot on the country's image, indicating incompatibility with the values of peace and democracy regarded as fundamental to the European integration project. But then in late 2002, the new government of the AKP (*Adalet ve Kalkınma Partisi*—Justice and Development Party) came out in open support of the reuniting of the island in the context of the UN's Annan Plan. This marked a dramatic shift in Turkey's Cyprus policy, indicating both a more pacific international stance and a relaxing of military control over foreign policy. This development was widely seen as signaling the depth of democratic change taking place in the country. Especially when contrasted with the rejection of the Plan by the Greek Cypriots, the new Cyprus policy had a beneficial impact on Turkey's image, suggesting Turkey was acquiring a more 'European' identity. This in turn helped to open the way for the December 2004 European Council decision to open accession negotiations.

However, the Greek Cypriot rejection of the Annan Plan in April 2004 dashed hopes that the EU external anchor would resolve the Cyprus conflict. Instead, EU involvement has so far only transformed the situation to a new impasse, with the Greek Cypriots inside the EU, the Turkish Cypriots outside and the island still divided. In this situation, Cyprus rapidly emerged as a major roadblock on Turkey's path to the EU. Partly this is due to the potential veto power wielded by the Greek Cypriot government now that it is an EU member. The spectre of former President Tassos Papadopoulos' proclaimed 64 opportunities to block Turkey's progress at the opening and closing of each technical chapter has

---

[1] K. Kirişci, 'Turkey's foreign policy in turbulent times', *Chaillot Paper*, No 92, Insitute for Security Studies, Paris, 2006, p. 8.

certainly haunted the negotiating table. But equally significant has been Turkey's non-recognition of an EU state, the internationally recognized Republic of Cyprus, and consequent refusal to open its harbours and airports to the latter's ships and planes. This has created an issue of Turkish non-compliance with legal obligations arising from the Turkey-EU customs union. As a direct result, the European Council decided in December 2006 not to open any of the negotiating chapters linked to the customs union until the Turkish government changes its policy.

This suggests that in recent years, the Cyprus issue has operated as both opportunity and constraint in Turkey's relations with the EU. The theme of this study is the three-way linkage between Turkey's Cyprus policy, its EU accession process and the domestic democratic transformation that the latter has promoted. The article aims to show how Turkey's 'Europeanisation' has affected one of its most delicate foreign policy issues, giving new content to a policy which was traditionally shaped by extremely sensitive nationalist perspectives and hard security content. This raises the question whether the evolution of Turkish policy on Cyprus can be regarded as an example of 'democratic peace', confirming the well-known theory that liberal democracies do not go to war with one another.

However, the article will also indicate that the interlinkage between Turkey's Cyprus policy and domestic democratisation has been a two-way process. During the delicate process of democratic transition, negative developments with regard to Cyprus have impacted on Turkey's domestic politics. When its initiatives on the Cyprus issue did not deliver the expected results, the AKP government was left more vulnerable to the charges coming from hard security circles, making it harder to proceed with democratic reform. In turn, this domestic backlash has left little margin for further flexibility in Turkey's Cyprus policy. The fluctuating credibility of Turkey's partnership with the EU has been a key factor in this process.

The article will proceed by first offering a framework of analysis, making reference to Europeanisation, conditionality and 'democratic peace theory'. The main body of the study follows, consisting of a diachronic examination of the impact of Europeanisation on Turkey's Cyprus policy. This is divided into three chronological periods, separated by two key events: the EU's 1999 Helsinki Council and the 2004 Annan Plan referenda in Cyprus. The final section seeks to draw conclusions from the case study, focusing on the themes of Europeanisation, conditionality and democratic peace theory.

Europeanisation, conditionality and democratic peace

'Europeanisation' describes the processes of transformation of the domestic structures of states as a result of European integration.[2] Initially defined by

---

[2]Among the extensive literature on Europeanisation, see in particular the following comprehensive edited volumes: T. Risse, J. Caporaso and M. Green Cowles (eds), *Transforming Europe: Europeanisation and Domestic Change*, Cornell University Press, NewYork, 2001; K. Featherstone and C. M. Radaelli (eds), *The Politics of Europeanisation*, Oxford University Press, Oxford, 2003; P. Graziano and M. P. Vink (eds), *Europeanisation: New Research Agendas*, Palgrave Macmillan, 2007.

Ladrech in terms of national adaptation to EU membership, where 'EC political and economic dynamics become part of the organisational logic of national politics and policy-making', 'Europeanisation' entails a shift from a national to a common European logic in many policy areas.[3] While the initial emphasis of Europeanisation studies was on institutional change and domestic policy formulation and implementation, it is now increasingly seen to apply to foreign policy as well.

In the case of EU member-states, the emphasis of the foreign policy Europeanisation literature is on the socialization effects of participation in European integration.[4] In the case of candidate states, the process is somewhat different. The chief mechanism, as Aydin and Acikmese also argue in this volume, is the conditionality applied during the accession process. In order for their candidacies to advance, applicant states are obliged to comply with the formal entry criteria stipulated by the EU, chief among which are the political criteria: the four established at the Copenhagen summit in 1993 (stability of democratic institutions, rule of law, respect for human and minority rights) and the 'good neighbourliness' criterion, added at the Helsinki summit in 1999.

Democratisation through the process of EU accession, as Oguzlu points out, requires not just establishment of a democratic regime but also the internalisation of the EU's identity.[5] Fundamental here are the view of the EU as a community based on democratic values[6] and the traditional self-perception of European integration as a peace project. The latter is clearly expressed, for example, in the preambles to the founding treaties of all three original European Communities in the 1950s and is also reflected in Karl Deutsch's concept of a security community, dating from the same era.[7] Becoming part of the EU thus implies that candidate states formulate and implement foreign policies in accordance with this identity and resultant EU interests—implying the pursuit of good neighbourly relations and the peaceful resolution of conflicts in accordance with international law.

In the 21st century, the idea that democracy promotion through conditionality can promote conflict resolution and create a zone of peace and security has been central to EU policy in Southeastern Europe. This is the basic belief driving the Stabilisation and Association Process in the Western Balkans, for example. This policy concept clearly reflects 'democratic peace theory', which posits a correlation between a state's level of democracy and its peaceful/co-operative foreign policy behaviour towards other democracies. Here, we will make brief reference to the debate in the academic literature around this theory.

---

[3]R. Ladrech, 'The Europeanisation of domestic politics and institutions: the case of France', *Journal of Common Market Studies*, 32(1), 1994, p. 69.

[4]E.g. M. E. Smith, 'Conforming to Europe: the domestic impact of EU foreign policy cooperation', *Journal of European Public Policy*, 7(4), 2000, pp. 616–620; B. Tonra, *The Europeanisation of National Foreign Policy: Dutch, Danish and Irish Foreign Policy in the European Union*, Ashgate, Aldershot, 2001, pp. 42–56; P. Rieker, *Europeanisation of National Security Identity: the EU and the Changing Security Identities of the Nordic States*, Routledge, London, 2006, pp. 51–63.

[5]T. Oguzlu, 'The impact of democratisation in the context of the EU accession process' on Turkish foreign policy', *Mediterranean Politics*, 9(1), 2004, p. 97.

[6]For perhaps the most eloquent expression of this, see the Declaration of the European Council at Laeken in 2001, www.consilium.europa.eu.

[7]K. W. Deutsch *et al.*, *Political Community and the North Atlantic Area: International Organisation in the Light of Historical Experience*, Princeton University Press, Princeton, 1957.

Following the Kantian logic of liberal internationalism, it has been claimed, notably by Doyle, that the increasing weight of public opinion, the establishment of institutional checks and balances, and the internalisation of democratic norms accompanying the democratisation process require more cautious, more rational, more co-operative and less costly outcomes in foreign policy making and implementation.[8] It is argued that in a democratising state, the power holders, in reconstructing their domestic identities through foreign policy practices, are constrained by the increasing involvement of societal actors in the policy-making process and their own expectations concerning re-election. While democratic institutions restrain political elites from engaging in reckless foreign policy behaviour, domestic norms of non-violent conflict resolution together with increasing pluralism, tolerance and rational debate in democratising societies, transform the foreign policy process.[9] Applied to the Turkish case, this would imply that a democratising Turkey would adopt a more compromising foreign policy style, a more multi-dimensional foreign policy-making process and more co-operative attitudes towards other democracies—suggesting it would also be easier to reach an accommodation over Cyprus.

Democratic peace theory has been contested, for example by Spiro, who used statistical surveys to question the correlation between democratisation and peace.[10] A more radical challenge came from Mansfield and Snyder, who underlined the necessity of qualifying these bold assessments of 'democratic peace theory' with specific case studies of countries involved in the democratisation process. They suggested that not only do democratisation processes not necessarily create conditions conducive to peaceful outcomes, but also that they may actually produce more warlike behaviour. For them,

> the problem is not that the mass public opinion in democratising states demonstrates unvarnished, persistent preferences for military adventures. On the contrary public opinion often starts off highly averse to war. Rather, elites exploit their power in the imperfect institutions of partial democracies to create *faits accomplis*, control political agendas, and shape the content of information media in ways that promote belligerent pressure-group lobbies or upwelling of militancy in the populace as a whole.[11]

With specific reference to Cyprus, Fiona B. Adamson, in a study published in 2001, claimed that the past history of the conflict appears to disprove democratic peace theory.[12] However, in another article published a year later, she suggested that the process of democratic consolidation taking place in the context of the EU

---

[8]M. Doyle, 'Kant liberal legacies and foreign affairs', *Philosophy and Public Affairs*, 12(3), 1983, pp. 205–235; M. Doyle, 'Liberalism and world politics', *American Political Science Review*, 80(4), 1986, pp. 1151–69.

[9]B. Russett, 'The democratic peace—and yet it moves', *International Security*, 19(4), 1993, pp. 164–175; J. Owen, 'How liberalism produces democratic peace', *International Security*, 19(2), 1994, pp. 87–125; T. Risse-Kappen, 'Democratic peace—warlike democracies? A social constructivist interpretation of the liberal argument', *European Journal of International Relations*, 1(4), 1995, pp. 491–517.

[10]D. Spiro, 'The insignificance of the liberal peace', *International Security*, 19(2), 1994, pp. 50–86.

[11]E. Mansfield and J. Snyder, 'Democratisation and the danger of war', *International Security*, 20(1), 1995, p. 7.

[12]F. Adamson, 'Democratisation and the domestic sources of foreign policy: Turkey in the 1974 Cyprus crisis', *Political Science Quarterly*, 116(2), 2001, pp. 299–303.

accession process might constitute a major departure. Occurring in an era of globalization in which Turkish elites have developed significant transnational links and interests, she noted that democratisation in the EU context has the potential to encourage the articulation of new identities and produce different outcomes.[13] Our article examines the extent to which this has been the case.

Status quo: Turkey's Cyprus policy pre-1999

For Turkey, the Cyprus problem, since its inception during the decolonisation process of 1950s, has never been an ordinary foreign policy issue. Instead, it has been defined as a 'national cause', due to the sense of ethnic kinship with the Turkish Cypriots. As such, it is an extremely sensitive question capable of rallying support across the Turkish political spectrum. The Cyprus question has had considerable impact on the internal dynamism of Turkish democracy, because of its high nationalist resonance and its use by hardline circles in Turkey as a populist tool.[14] It has been used by Turkish political elites to incite nationalism and populism and divert public attention from social and economic problems. In particular, it has served belligerent pressure groups inside and outside military circles, whose aim has been to manipulate and limit any democratic transition which would bring an end to their own dominant position. As Kaliber puts, in 'the pendulum swing between political normalisation and securitisation, the Cyprus issue has served as a trump card in the hands of the securitisers'.[15]

From the Turkish viewpoint, the treaties of 1959 and 1960, establishing the independence of the Republic of Cyprus from British colonial rule, were satisfactory as they established constitutional mechanisms and guarantees for the minority Turkish Cypriots (18% of the island's population) in relation to the majority Greek Cypriots (80%). However, the independence settlement, challenged by the Greek Cypriots, broke down in 1963, with the intercommunal clashes resulting in the establishment of a UN peacekeeping mission on the island. The continuing tension culminated with the July 1974 coup against the government of the Republic of Cyprus, initiated by the military junta then in power in Athens. This was followed by the Turkish counter intervention, with the Turkish government citing its rights to intervene as one of the guarantor powers of the independence settlement. But the military intervention of 1974 and subsequent permanent presence of Turkish armed forces in the northern part of the island were not accepted as legitimate by the international community, which also rejected the unilateral declaration of independence by the 'Turkish Republic of Northern Cyprus' ('TRNC') in 1983. This left Turkey in the difficult position of being the only state to recognize the otherwise internationally isolated Turkish Cypriot regime. At the same time, Turkey also remained alone within the international community in not according diplomatic recognition to the post-1974 Greek Cypriot governments.

[13]F. B. Adamson, 'Democratisation in Turkey, EU Enlargement and the regional dynamics of the Cyprus conflict', in T. Diez (ed.), *The European Union and the Cyprus Conflict: Modern Conflict, Postmodern Union*, Manchester University Press, Manchester and New York, 2002, pp. 163–180.

[14]N. Kızılyürek, *Milliyetçilik Kıskacında Kıbrıs*, İletişim, İstanbul, 2003; M. Hasgüler, *Kıbrıs'ta Enosis ve Taksim Politikalarının Sonu*, Alfa, İstanbul, 2007.

[15]A. Kaliber, 'Securing the ground through securitized 'foreign policy': the Cyprus case', *Security Dialogue*, 36(3), 2005, p. 333.

From 1974 onwards, the EC clearly placed the Cyprus question on the agenda of Turkish-EC relations, then based on the Association Agreement signed in 1963.[16] But despite the references in the Association treaty to the possibility of eventual full Turkish membership, in the mid-1970s there was no credible accession prospect in sight. Economic relations were still in the long-term preparatory stage preceding the planned move to a customs union. Disappointment with the economic functioning of the Association[17], combined with the preference of significant domestic interest groups for a policy of import substitution, had significantly reduced the EC's 'power of attraction'. Meanwhile, from the Turkish viewpoint, the Community's credibility as a potential actor in conflict resolution in Cyprus had been fatally damaged by its decision to proceed with the accession application submitted in 1975 by Greece, the other major party to the dispute. The Community's lack of leverage in Ankara was graphically underlined when the Turkish government unilaterally froze the Association in 1978.

The next stage in the drama was the EC's official suspension of the Association following the Turkish military coup of 1980. This was not the first time that democratic considerations had influenced Turkish-EC relations. In 1960, the negotiations for the Association Agreement had been temporarily suspended after another military coup.[18] But when the Agreement was finally negotiated in 1963, it did not include any reference to political conditions as a prerequisite for the progress of relations. However, following the pathbreaking precedent of democratic conditionality established by the EC's limitation of the Greek Association during the junta of 1967–74, the 1982 suspension of the Turkish Association explicitly linked Turkey's EC prospects to the existence of a democratic government in Ankara. The Turkish accession application submitted in 1987, reflecting a shift towards an externally-orientated economic strategy, might have been expected to open a new era, offering possibilities for EC influence over Turkey's Cyprus policy. This did not occur, due to the EC's exceptionally lukewarm response, with the European Commission's 1989 *Opinion* making it clear that accession negotiations were not on the agenda for the immediate future.

During the late 1980s and early 1990s, Turkey's stance was based on rejecting any linkage between the Cyprus issue and relations with the EC. For instance, responding to a May 1988 EP resolution, emphasising the Cyprus issue as the most serious obstacle to Turkey-EU relations, Foreign Minister Mesut Yilmaz withdrew from an Association Council meeting, stating that the Turkish government would not accept any linkage of these two topics.[19] But then two

---

[16]E.g. see the European Parliament Resolutions of 19 September 1975 and 28 April 1976, in which the EP stressed its hopes for more 'practical results' from the intercommunal talks and called for the 'necessary solutions' to be worked out 'as soon as possible by peaceful means'. Reprinted in Republic of Cyprus Press and Information Office, *European Stand on the Cyprus Problem*, Nicosia, 1998, pp. 56–60.

[17]See introduction by Verney to this volume.

[18]M. Müftüler-Bac, *Turkey's Relations with a Changing Europe*, Manchester University Press, Manchester, 1997, p. 55.

[19]*European Parliament* (1988), 'Resolution on Turkey', 20 May 1988, pp. 205–207; M. A. Birand, *Turkiye'nin Avrupa Macerasi (1959–1999)*, Dogan Kitap, Istanbul, 2000, p. 479.

major developments in late 1993 altered the stakes for Turkey, upgrading the significance of both democracy and Cyprus for its EU prospects.

First, the introduction of formal political criteria for EU membership made it clear that the existence of a democratically elected government was no longer sufficient. Instead, a significant programme of domestic reform would be required if Turkey was ever to enter the EU. Second, in its *Opinion* on the membership application submitted by the Greek Cypriot government three years earlier, the European Commission recognised Cyprus as 'eligible for EU membership'. The prospect of ultimate Cypriot accession became more concrete with the June 1994 Corfu summit statement that the next round of Enlargement would include Cyprus and Malta and the March 1995 Council decision to open negotiations with Cyprus six months after the conclusion of the Intergovern-mental Conference due to open the following year. Subsequently, EU concern at the prospect of admitting Cyprus while the island remained partitioned—meaning that Turkish military forces would be stationed on EU territory—made the resolution of the Cyprus conflict a central issue for Turkey-EU relations, with the European Parliament playing a particularly active role in maintaining this linkage.[20]

However, for most of the 1990s, EU pressure on Turkey both to democratise and to change its Cyprus policy seemed to have little effect. Essentially this appears to be because the EU was prepared to offer little in return. The customs union agreement, signed in December 1995, was a development already pro-mised 30 years ago, under the Association. Moreover, it was now promoted by many in the EU as a potential alternative to offering Turkey a closer relationship. It is therefore hardly surprising that it does not seem to have had an impact on Turkey's Cyprus policy.

Instead, Turkish political elites continued to deem the Cyprus dispute as lying within the realm of Turkey's national interests and adopted a cynical attitude towards the involvement of external actors in the issue. Characteristically, during the parliamentary debates on the customs union, the question whether Turkey had made concessions on Cyprus in order to conclude the agreement occupied centre stage.[21] Moreover, the customs union agreement was followed by one of the worst incidents on Cyprus since 1974. The violence which occurred on the 'Green Line' in September 1996, resulting in the deaths of two Greek Cypriots, was captured on film and broadcast around Europe, seriously damaging the image of the Turkish side. This coincided with a difficult period for Turkish democracy, with the formation of a coalition government including the Islamist Welfare Party in 1996, followed by its downfall as a result of National Security Council intervention in February 1997.

The period before and after the Luxembourg summit in December 1997 constituted one of the worst ebbs in EU-Turkey relations. At the summit, the EU formally recognized as candidates ten Central and East European states—all of which had submitted their membership applications after Turkey. The EU also

---

[20]E.g. see the memoir by Pauline Green, leader of the EP Socialist Group, P. Green and R. Collins, *Embracing Cyprus: The Path to Unity in the New Europe*, I. B.Tauris, New York, 2003, pp. 27–41. For more on the EP's role, see S. Verney, 'From consensus to conflict: changing perceptions of the Cyprus issue in the European Parliament, 1995–2005', in T. Diez and N. Tocci, *Cyprus: A Conflict at the Crossroads*, Manchester University Press, Manchester, 2009, forthcoming.

[21]Turkish Grand National Assembly, *Parliamentary Debates*, 21 February 1995.

agreed to open accession negotiations with six governments, including the Greek Cypriots. In contrast, Turkey was only declared 'eligible for membership' and the EU made no commitment with respect to Turkish accession. Instead, on offer was 'a European strategy for Turkey' involving 'enhanced cooperation'. Even this would be conditional on peaceful settlement of disputes in accordance with international law, including support for a political settlement in Cyprus.[22] The Turkish government reacted strongly, warning that if the EU continued with the Greek Cypriot accession process, Turkey would speed up the process of full integration with the 'TRNC'.[23]

The policy of negating any linkage between the Cyprus issue and relations with the EU continued in the lead-up to the Helsinki Council in 1999. On 8 December, three days before the summit, Foreign Minister Ismail Cem stated that Turkey 'rejects the idea of any explicit conditions concerning relations with Greece or the Cyprus issue'.[24] Turkish resistance was so strong that the EU, going beyond the normal procedure, sent Javier Solana, High Representative for the CFSP and Gunter Verheugen, Commissioner responsible for Enlargement, to Ankara on the night of 10 December. Their mission was to hand over a letter signed by the incumbent President of the Council of the EU, officially informing Prime Minister Ecevit of the unanimous EU decision to grant Turkey the status of candidate State, 'on an equal footing' with the other candidates.

Change, 1999–2004

As Mehmet Ugur has noted, the Helsinki summit radically transformed the nature of Turkey-EU relations by addressing the incomplete nature of the contract between Turkey and the EU. The decision to grant Turkey official candidate status provided an element which had been missing for the previous four decades—a contractual agreement based on the effective monitoring of Turkish convergence towards EU norms, and backed by EU compliance with its own obligations towards Turkey.[25] Helsinki had a crucial impact on Turkey's democratisation, as the degree of ambiguity in EU–Turkey relations started to decrease, the EU's commitments to Turkey became clearer and pro-EU reformists in Turkey were empowered. It was also significant for the Cyprus question, as the introduction of the 'good neighbourliness' criterion at Helsinki formally established linkage between the progress of Turkey-EU relations and the peaceful resolution of problems with its neighbours on the basis of the UN Charter.

The impact of Helsinki was more immediately apparent in the domestic sphere. The *National Programme* issued in March 2001 was followed by a series of three reform packages, constituting major challenges to the Turkish political system by extending individual liberties, freedom of expression and the recognition of non-Turkish ethnic identities. In contrast, with regard to Cyprus

---

[22]*Presidency Conclusions*, European Council, Luxemburg, 12 December 1997.

[23]In order to show determination to continue special relations with 'TRNC', Turkey signed a 'Protocol on Functional and Structural Cooperation', with 'TRNC' on 13 Janury 1998. For full text of the Protocol, see, *Perceptions*, 1998, 3(1).

[24]*Turkish Daily News*, 9 December 1999.

[25]M. Ugur, 'Europeanisation and convergence via incomplete contracts? The case of Turkey', in *South European Society and Politics*, 5(2), 2000, pp. 217–242.

policy, there initially appeared to have been no change. The position of the three-party coalition which governed in 1999-2002 was laid out in an article by Foreign Minister, Ismail Çem, published in the *International Herald Tribune* in March 2002. Çem reaffirmed Ankara's official backing for Rauf Denktaş, the long-lasting leader of the Turkish Cypriot community, usually regarded as a hardliner. The article stated that a settlement on the island would require 'the confirmation of two equal separate states, each as a sovereign entity, forming through an agreement a new partnership state'.[26] The latter implied a confederal solution rather than the federal framework promoted by the UN.

However, post-Helsinki, a significant section of the Turkish governing elite was becoming increasingly conscious of the fact that the Cyprus problem appeared as the main obstacle for Turkey on the way to EU accession.[27] In late 2002, the Turkish attitude towards accepting such a linkage began to shift. Two key events occurred in November. The first was the election of the AKP (*Adalet ve Kalkınma Partisi*—Justice and Development Party) on a manifesto pledging the fulfilment of the Copenhagen criteria and the adoption of an anti-status quo approach to foreign policy issues, including Cyprus and Greek-Turkish relations.[28] The second was the publication of the UN's Annan Plan, proposing a detailed framework for a solution to the Cyprus conflict in the framework of the accession of a united island to the EU.

Once in power, the new AKP government proceeded to speed up the process of domestic democratisation with a whole series of reforms, including sweeping changes to the previously institutionalised role of the military in politics.[29] As the military's political grip became less intense, Turkey's foreign policy objectives—including Turkey-EU relations with their increasing domestic repercussions—became open to pressures outside the traditional foreign policy establishment.[30] With regard to Cyprus, even before winning the election, the AKP had declared its support for the 'Belgian formula' of a loose federation of strong constituent states, which constitutes the basic framework of the Annan Plan. This was a significant divergence from previous policies that had been a constant given for mainstream parties of both left and right.

The original UN aim had been to secure agreement on the Plan before the Copenhagen Summit in December 2002, but this proved impossible, due particularly to the negative attitude of the 'TRNC' leadership. It was in this context that the Copenhagen Council formally closed accession negotiations with Cyprus, opening the way for EU entry but with the application of the *acquis communautaire* suspended in the north of the island pending a settlement. The Council also called for the northern part of Cyprus to be brought closer to the Union. With regard to Turkey, the Council did not decide to move to the next stage in the accession process. However, it made a commitment that 'if the

---

[26]I. Cem, 'A common vision for Cyprus', *International Herald Tribune*, 14 March 2002.

[27]H. Cemal, 'AB yolunda sahici sorun Kıbrıs ya patlarsa', *Milliyet* (Turkish Daily), 20 October 2001.

[28]N. Göle, 'AKP hem kendi dönüşüyor hem Türkiye'yi dönüştürüyor.', *Vatan* (Turkish Daily), 1 October 2003.

[29]M. Müftuler-Bac, 'Turkey's political reforms and the impact of the European Union', *South European Society & Politics*, 10(1), April 2005.

[30]S. Ayata 'Changes in domestic politics and the foreign policy of the AK Party', in L. G. Martin and D. Keridis (eds), *The Future of Turkish Foreign Policy*, The MIT Press, Cambridge, Massachusetts, 2004, pp. 268–274.

December 2004 European Council [in Brussels] decides that Turkey has fulfilled the Copenhagen political criteria, the negotiations will be opened without delay'.[31]

The new Turkish government interpreted this promise in positive terms, thus opening new prospects for a more EU-oriented foreign policy. There was a growing understanding among opinion leaders that Cyprus had been the cause of many troubles, including the tensions that Turkish diplomacy had suffered from in the international arena since the mid-1970s. Meanwhile, there were new societal pressures for policy change, both in Turkey—where sections of business and the media linked the success of Turkey's accession project to the Cyprus question[32]—and the 'TRNC'.

On the eve of the Copenhagen Summit and in its immediate aftermath, many Turkish Cypriots reacted strongly to Denktaş's reluctance to seriously negotiate the Annan Plan.[33] The UN's new deadline of 28 February 2003 for agreement on the Plan was presented as the last chance for the Turkish Cypriots to share in the peace and prosperity of the EU alongside the Greek Cypriots.[34] Indicative of the new climate were the mass demonstrations on 14 January 2003 in which one-third of the population in North Cyprus participated.[35] The demands were clear: resolution of the Cyprus problem on the basis of the Annan Plan and participation in Cyprus' EU accession.

This societal dissent in northern Cyprus, itself encouraged by the emergence of the new government in Ankara, in turn exerted pressure on the latter to change its Cyprus policy. In this context, Turkey's well-established Cyprus policy showed signs of major reformulation,[36] with the Turkish government agreeing to the continuation of inter-communal talks on the Annan Plan. The change in government policy evoked strong reactions from the hardliners, who claimed this would only serve to weaken Denktaş's position at the negotiating table.[37] The tension between Denktaş and the AKP government became more acute, as the latter shifted further away from Turkey's traditional Cyprus policy.[38] In response, Denktaş claimed that he had been stabbed in the back,[39] talked about treason to the 'national cause', and asked Turkey to find someone else to sign the deal.[40] Meanwhile, the Turkish military, although remaining very active behind the scenes, refrained from entering into open confrontation with the government.

---

[31]*European Council Conclusions*, Copenhagen, 12–13 December 2002.

[32]H. Cemal, 'Kıbrıs'ta son şans: 28 February!', *Milliyet* (Turkish Daily), 17 December 2002.

[33]'Kıbrıslı Türkler Patladı', *Radikal* (Turkish Daily), 11 January 2003.

[34]J. Ker-Lindsay, *EU Accession and UN Peacemaking in Cyprus*, Palgrave, New York, 2005, pp. 44–46.

[35]'Dört Kıbrıslıdan biri mitingde', Milliyet (Turkish Daily), 15 January 2003; 'Turkish Cypriots rally for UN Plan', *The Guardian*, 15 January 2003.

[36]'Kıbrıs'ta yeni politika: Geleneksel siyasette değişikliğe gidildiği Dışişleri tarafından resmen açıklandı', *Cumhuriyet* (Turkish Daily), 9 January 2003; 'Dışilerinden bir gaf daha. Denktaş'a lider dediler', *Cumhuriyet* (Turkish Daily), 11 January 2003.

[37]'Denktas complains protest demos hurt his negotiating position', *Turkish Daily News*, 14 Janury 2003.; Ş.S. Gürel 'Tehdit', *Cumhuriyet* (Turkish Daily), 11 January 2003.

[38]'Denktaş söz düellosunda', *Radikal* (Turkish Daily), 3 January 2003.

[39]'Denktaş: Beni arkamdan Hançerlediler', Inteview with F. Bila, *Milliyet* (Turkish Daily), 19 January 2003.

[40]'Denktaş: Türkiye milli davadan vazgeçtiyse biri imzayı atar', *Milliyet* (Turkish Daily), 26 January 2003.

In fact, the military response was conflicting. On the one hand, the army initially forced the government to tone down its policy declarations and state that Turkey's Cyprus policy remained essentially the same.[41] On the other, there were indications that the military had begun to devise a new strategy, favouring bilateral negotiations as opposed to rejecting the new UN plan outright. Turkish commentators started to talk about 'a new security strategy', taking account of the fact that while Cyprus was significant, the EU was also important for Turkey both strategically and in terms of domestic stability.[42] From December 2002, there were already indications that the military might eventually acknowledge that the Cyprus issue had become a problem for Turkey and that the 'solution had to come from outside'.[43]

However, during 2003, progress towards a deal within the Annan Plan framework was rather limited. Although negotiations were resumed on 15 January, neither the presentation of the second revision of the Plan on 26 February, nor Kofi Annan's meeting with both sides on 10–11 March in Hague produced the expected steps towards a solution. The then newly elected Greek Cypriot President, Tassos Papadopoulos, while having serious reservations about the Plan, agreed to put it to a popular vote.[44] In contrast, Denktaş simply resorted to his well known delaying tactics, continuing to suggest confidence building measures instead of negotiating the Plan. As a result, when Kofi Annan issued his report on his good offices in Cyprus on 1 April, he blamed Denktaş for the collapse of the talks. On 16 April, the Republic of Cyprus signed its Treaty of Acccession to the EU, dramatically increasing the Greek Cypriots' negotiating power *vis a vis* the Turkish Cypriots. Although the Green Line dividing the two communities on the island was opened on 23 April, resulting in a visible improvement in the overall climate, there was little prospect for a resumption of negotiations.

Because of his uncompromising stance, Denktaş came under intense international pressures, and was severely criticised both within the Turkish Cypriot community and in Turkey.[45] The Turkish government also came under EU pressure, with both the European Commission's regular report on Turkey and its 2003 strategy paper stating that 'the absence of a settlement could become a serious obstacle to Turkey's EU aspirations'.[46] International pressure further encouraged those societal forces in both Turkey and the 'TRNC' who favoured a more concessionary line on Cyprus.

The domestic pressures on both the 'TRNC' and Turkish governments increased with the victory of the pro-solution parties in the Turkish Cypriot legislative elections in December 2003.[47] While Denktaş as President remained

---

[41]'Org. Özkök: Yeni Kıbrıs Planı Kötü', *Milliyet* (Turkish Daily), 11 December 2002.

[42]H. Cemal, 'Asker kişi gözüyle Kıbrıs', *Milliyet* (Turkish Daily), 18 January 2003.

[43]Ugur, 2003: 180.

[44]Some commentators later interpreted his stance as an intelligent diplomatic maneuvere to secure the signing of the EU accession treaty a few weeks later.

[45]J. Ker-Lindsay, *EU Accession and UN Peacemaking in Cyprus*, Palgrave, New York, 2005, pp. 50–70.

[46]Commission of the European Communities, *Strategy Paper and Report of the European Commission on the Progress towards Accession of Bulgaria, Romania and Turkey*, 5 October 2003 (final), p.16.

[47]On the elections, see A. Çarkoğlu and A. Sözen (2004), 'The Turkish Cypriot general elections of December 2003: setting the stage for resolving the Cyprus conflict?', *South European Society and Politics*, 9(3), pp. 122–136.

the official negotiator, the formation of a coalition government led by M.A. Talat was a further factor encouraging the Turkish government to adopt a constructive stance towards the Annan Plan. At this point, the AKP government in Turkey, backed by a significant section of the governing elite, including sectors of the media, business and the civil and military bureaucracy, decided to support new inter-communal negotiations for a comprehensive settlement based on the Plan. The decision of the Turkish National Security Council on 22 January 2004 to return to the negotiating table was followed by new talks. The final version of the Plan, Annan V, presented on 31 March, was put to referenda within both communities on the island a few weeks later, in order to pre-empt the accession of a divided Cyprus, due to take place on 1 May 2004.

Paralysis, post-2004

The referenda of 24 April 2004 marked a crucial break in the Cyprus problem. The Turkish Cypriots, long seen as a major obstacle to a solution, voted in favour of the Plan by a 64.9% majority while the Greek Cypriots rejected it with a majority of 75.8%.[48] The Annan Plan's creators had assumed that Denktaş and the 'Turkish establishment', who for many years had been perceived as the main obstacles to the unification of the island, would be its main opponents. Although Denktaş maintained his ardent opposition to the Plan to the end, Turkey's position, as indicated above, had been gradually transformed. Despite severe criticism of the Plan in strong circles in Turkey who regard the Cyprus issue as a 'national cause', the AKP government supported it and disassociated itself from Denktaş—a crucial break from the policy of previous governments. Moreover, there was an impressive media campaign in support of the Plan in Turkey. In contrast, Greek Cypriot President Papadopoulos made an emotive televised speech urging his compatriots to vote against the Plan. The latter's supporters, including Enlargement Commissioner Verheugen, were denied access to Cypriot television in order to present their views. These events overturned longheld perceptions of Turkey and the Turkish Cypriots as the main obstacle to conflict resolution.

The primary Turkish gain was that in discarding the label of the main opponent to Cyprus' reunification, Turkey overcame one of the main obstacles to opening its own accession negotiations.[49] At the European Council meeting in December 2004, the Council 'welcomed the positive contribution of Turkey to the UN efforts for the settlement of Cyprus Problem' and agreed that it 'sufficiently' fulfilled the Copenhagen political criteria to begin accession negotiations in October 2005.[50]

However, the opening of negotiations was followed by a decline in popular support for EU membership within Turkey. This had also occurred in the central and East European states which joined the EU in 2004 and can be partly attributed to the dynamics of the negotiating process. But in the Turkish case, this

---

[48]For an analysis of the two referenda, see C. Christophorou, 'The vote for a united Cyprus deepens divisions: The 24 April 2004 referenda in Cyprus', *South European Society & Politics*, 10(1), pp. 85–104.

[49]'Turkey emerges as talks winner', *Financial Times*, 2 April, 2004, p. 2; 'Cyprus vote offers Turkey Silver Lining', *The Wall Street Journal Europe*, 26 April 2004, p. 1.

[50]European Council Conclusions, Brussels, 16–17 December 2004.

trend was reinforced by the declining credibility of the relationship with the EU. A particular cause for disaffection was the manifest reluctance of some EU members, notably France and Austria, to proceed with the Turkish accession process, despite the commitments made at Helsinki and Copenhagen. The December 2004 Council decision was preceded by a heated intra-EU debate in which Turkey's European nature—and hence qualification for EU membership—was repeatedly publicly challenged. Subsequently, Austria in particular fought a rearguard action, maintaining a threat to veto until just hours before the official opening of negotiations on 3 October 2005. Anger with what was seen as a discriminatory attitude towards Turkey was compounded by disillusion concerning Turkey's prospects of ever joining the EU.

Moreover, the Cyprus question itself played a key role, as the situation which developed after April 2004 proved a complete disappointment to the Turkish side. Despite the significant policy shift on the part of both the Turkish government and the Turkish Cypriots, the latter were excluded from the EU as a result of the Greek Cypriots' vote against the Annan Plan. The Greek Cypriot government not only joined the EU as the sole representative of the divided island, but once within the EU gained a potential veto over relations with the Turkish Cypriots. Two days after the failed referenda, the EU's General Affairs Council declared that it was 'determined to end the isolation of the Turkish Cypriot community'. But following the Republic of Cyprus' EU entry just a few days later, this goal proved hard to implement. It took almost two years and much debate before a regulation providing financial aid to the Turkish Cypriots was finally approved in February 2006. Meanwhile, at the time of writing, four years after the referenda, the proposed 'Direct Trade Regulation' remains stalled in the face of Greek Cypriot opposition.

Further aggravating the situation, from 2005 onwards the Turkish government came under increasing pressure to recognise the Greek Cypriot government in order to fulfil its legal obligations under the 1995 Turkey-EU customs union. This would be a major concession on a sensitive 'national cause', implying a complete reversal of Turkey's post-1974 Cyprus policy. It was called for at a time when the EU had not only proved unable to end the Turkish Cypriots' international isolation, but also appeared unwilling to maintain its commitment to eventual Turkish accession. The result was to turn the Cyprus question—once again—into a particularly potent tool for groups in Turkey threatened by domestic change.

The apparent policy failure in Cyprus thus helped to fuel a domestic nationalist backlash, seriously weakening the government's possibility of proceeding with domestic reform. Meanwhile, with euroscepticism rapidly rising post-2004, the argument that reform was necessary to promote the country's EU accession process lost some of its persuasive power. The consequences are clearly noted in the European Commission's reports on Turkey. From 2005 onwards, the constant refrain has been that 'the pace of change has slowed', accompanied by a call for 'more concrete achievements'.[51] With the reform effort weakened and domestic 'securitisers' once again gaining the upper hand, the Turkish

---

[51]European Commission, 2005 *Enlargement Strategy Paper*, COM(2005)561 final p. 5; *Enlargement Strategy and Main Challenges 2006–7*, COM (2006)649, p. 11; *Enlargement Strategy and Main Challenges 2007–8*, COM (2007)663 final, p. 8.

government's margins for flexibility on Cyprus were greatly reduced. Meanwhile, it sometimes also resorted to the use of nationalism itself as an attractive populist tool to gain support in the developing domestic conflict with the anti-reform coalition.

A vicious circle began to develop. As relations between Turkey and Cyprus were not normalised, EU pressures on Turkey increased and the Turkish stance hardened towards Cyprus. For example, in December 2005, the Turkish government vetoed Cyprus' application to the International Wassenaar Arrangement on Export Controls for Conventional Arms and Dual-Use Technologies.[52] Turkey also insisted that Cyprus be excluded from EU-NATO strategic cooperation in crisis management conducted in the framework of the EU's European Security and Defence Policy. A few weeks later, Turkey refused to open its ports and airports to ships and aircraft operating under the Cypriot flag.[53] The more pacific foreign policy image acquired through the 2004 support for the Annan Plan has subsequently been increasingly overshadowed by these later developments.

While the tension over Cyprus encouraged predictions that Turkey was heading for a 'train wreck' in its accession negotiations, this prospect seemed to have been averted at the December 2006 European Council. The latter effectively limited the potential damage from the Cyprus problem by excluding further progress only in those negotiating chapters directly related to the customs union, pending Turkish recognition of the Republic of Cyprus. However, given the domestic political conjuncture, the Council decision, by underlining once again the explicit linkage between Turkish accession and concessions on Cyprus, may have further weakened the government in the domestic arena.

Since then, domestic tensions have escalated, with a growing confrontation between the government and its opponents. A crisis in spring 2007 was triggered by the judiciary's rejection of the governing party's right to propose a nominee from among its own ranks as presidential candidate. During the tense period that ensued, the Cyprus issue again became an important instrument of belligerent lobbies, including the military, as a tool for intervening in the political process and silencing the pro-reformist and democratic coalition. Although the AKP, with its convincing July electoral victory, initially appeared to have triumphed, a new phase of crisis opened with a fresh judicial challenge in early 2008. With the legality of the governing party itself in question as a result, the possibility of bold moves on the Cyprus question appears non-existent. Instead, whatever the outcome of the current Supreme Court case, a reversion to old certainties on the Cyprus problem appears the most likely option.

Europeanisation, credible commitments and democratic peace

Our case study of the Europeanisation of Turkey's Cyprus policy suggests some interesting conclusions. Firstly, it appears to provide confirmation of the theory of 'democratic peace'. In the early years of the 21st century, domestic democratisation in Turkey was accompanied by the formulation of a new revisionist stand on a major national issue. The AKP government's support for the Annan Plan overturned an entrenched policy, in place for more than a quarter century.

---

[52]'Turkey vetoes Greek-Cypriots in Wassenaar', *Abhaber.com*, 16 December 2005.
[53]'Turkish ban on Cypriot-flagged ships stirs new trouble', *EU Observer*, 28 December 2005.

As a result, it changed perceptions of Turkey—at least temporarily. From one of the main obstacles to lasting peace in Cyprus, Turkey briefly appeared as one of the pro-solution parties.

The second conclusion concerns the particular mechanisms of Europeanisation at work in this particular case. It is clear that the process of EU Enlargement acted as the catalyst for this change. Without the latter, there seemed no reason for any of the parties to shift their positions at this point, given that by the early 2000s, the Cyprus conflict had already remained frozen for several decades. However, Enlargement provided incentives for a reassessment, because it concerned not only Turkey's own accession prospects, but also those of the Republic of Cyprus. If the latter preceded the former—as in fact happened—then Turkey's accession process would run the risk of a future Cypriot veto.

Meanwhile, central to Enlargement was the process of conditionality. As Heather Grabbe has shown, conditionality allows the EU to act as a gatekeeper, controlling access to the next stage of the process according to the candidate state's conformity with preordained criteria.[54] In this case, the EU had been particularly clear about its expectations concerning a peaceful resolution of the Cyprus problem—underlining the point with the formal establishment of the 'good neighbourliness' criterion in 1999. But while the accession 'carrot' was undoubtedly effective in encouraging change in Turkey's Cyprus policy, this does not mean that the latter was simply a result of strategic calculation, designed to facilitate Turkey's move to the next stage on the accession path.

Enlargement not only altered the stakes but also changed the context of Turkish policymaking on the Cyprus question. The latter had formerly been the *domaine reservée* of the military and a narrow political elite in Turkey, acting in conjunction with the Denktaş leadership in the 'TRNC'. But EU conditionality, operating as a powerful lever for Turkish democratisation, impacted directly in this sphere. Its consequences included a reduced role for the military within the National Security Council and the opening up of the policy making process to a broader range of actors beyond the NSC. Meanwhile, the fear of EU exclusion radically altered the balance-of-forces among the Turkish Cypriots, while at the same time activating new social forces in Turkey. In both cases, the result was the mobilization of pro-accession coalitions, calling for greater societal participation in policy making and identifying their interests with a more conciliatory line on the Cyprus question. The outcome was to weaken the 'securitisers', providing the Turkish government with new margins for foreign policy flexibility. Thus, our second conclusion is that in our Turkish case, the key to policy change lay in the process of Enlargement through conditionality. The latter operated in a dual fashion. On the one hand, it worked through the immediate pressures exerted via the 'good neighbourliness' criterion and on the other, more indirectly but with important impact, through the democracy-promoting criteria established at Copenhagen.

Our third conclusion, confirming the findings of other researchers, is that EU conditionality is most effective when it is backed by credible EU commitments. During the first chronological period examined in our study, Turkey's relations with the EC\EU entered a phase of deepening. Following the limitation of the

---

[54]H. Grabbe, 'Europeanisation goes east: power and uncertainty in the EU accession process', in Featherstone and Radaelli, *The Politics of Europeanisation*, op.cit., pp. 303–327.

1963 Association Agreement first by one side and then by the other in 1978\1982, the reactivation of relations in the mid-1980s was followed by the 1987 accession application and the contraction of the customs union agreement in 1995. However, these developments did not seem to have any significant impact on the country's Cyprus policy. The EC\EU was simply unable to exert sufficient power of attraction to bring about policy change until it accepted Turkey as a candidate state on an equal footing with other candidates. The Helsinki decision of 1999 was then reinforced by the Copenhagen Council in 2002. This strengthened the EU commitment by providing a specific two-year time frame for opening the negotiations—a period well within the electoral cycle of the newly-elected government. The effects of this concrete promise on the implementation of domestic reform were recorded in the European Commission's 2004 regular report. It was noted that 'following decades of sporadic progress', the two years since 2002 had seen 'a substantial convergence in Turkey towards European standards'.[55] In turn, as already seen, domestic democratisation was a key factor in changing Cyprus policy.

Sadly, these conclusions, derived from the period preceding the Annan Plan referenda of April 2004, appear to be confirmed in the latter's aftermath. The interlinkage between Europeanisation, democratisation and foreign policy change was underlined post-2004, when problems in one sphere impacted so immediately on the others and the virtuous circle began to go into reverse. The result was a negative feedback reaction. Negative input from the Cyprus problem combined with less credible EU commitments to reduce incentives for both democratic reform and 'good neighbourliness', in turn leading to more negative output on the Cyprus question.

With regard to 'democratic peace theory', the Turkish case seems to corroborate the point made by Mansfield and Snyder, concerning the necessity of making a distinction between weak\unconsolidated and mature\consolidated democracies. Our Turkish study provides a good example of how in the former case, democracy may not necessarily produce peaceful foreign policy outcomes. Instead, domestic elites may resort to nationalism and populism as a means of political manipulation to divert the country's agenda from democratisation.

Besides its theoretical conclusions, our study clearly has policy implications for EU attempts to promote 'democratic peace' in regions such as the Western Balkans or the European Neighbourhood Policy area. As the Turkish case shows, the Europeanisation process is not linear. On the contrary, it is controversial, delicate, and carries a constant risk of failure or spill back from its original purposes. The example of Cyprus policy suggests that Europeanisation is not a structural but a conjunctural process, largely dependent on time and circumstances. It also underlines the influence of the EU's own role as a factor for Europeanisation success or failure.

The problem in the Turkish case was not only that EU involvement in the Cyprus problem failed to achieve conflict resolution, but also that the accession of the Republic of Cyprus meant the latter gained a potential veto over EU relations with both Turkey and the Turkish Cypriots. In this context, the EU seemed unable significantly to improve the lot of the Turkish Cypriots, while Turkey's

---

[55]Commission of the European Communities, *2004 Regular Report on Turkey's Progress Towards Accession*, SEC(2004)1201, p. 15.

non-recognition of the Greek Cypriot government developed into a major source of tension and pressure. Above all, however, the Turkish government was asked to make fundamental changes to its Cyprus policy in the name of an accession process which the EU side seemed increasing to be calling into question. The importance of credible commitments became particularly apparent when the EU seemed unable to provide them. The lessons for EU policy with regard to other countries, such as Serbia or the Ukraine, are obvious.

The Cyprus conflict and Turkey's European road

In some respects, the Europeanisation of Turkey's Cyprus policy can be seen as a paradigm of Turkey-EU relations. For at least three and a half decades, Turkey's institutional relationship with the EC\EU, while supposedly bringing the two sides gradually closer, did not affect policy in this sphere. Although the Helsinki summit changed the climate, the Europeanisation of Cyprus policy essentially began post-2002 and took place on different levels. Firstly, Europeanisation influenced political institutions, giving the elected government greater autonomy in relation to the National Security Council. Secondly, it altered policymaking processes, involving new actors and the shaping of a reform coalition, including a significant section of Turkish Cypriot society. Thirdly, this led to new policy outputs, in this case entailing a reassessment of the former stand on Cyprus. And fourthly, in the process, it impacted on identities, with Turkey apparently moving closer to the 'European' values of peace and democracy. But when Europeanisation of the problem failed to produce a quick resolution, the new Cyprus policy rapidly reached impasse. This reflected the way in which the whole Turkish Europeanisation project seemed to be in jeopardy, so soon after it had begun.

For Turkey's road to European Union—the theme of this book—the frozen Cyprus conflict constitutes a major structural obstacle. This is not only due to such practical considerations as voting coalitions within EU institutions. It is above all because the Turkish military presence in Cyprus is considered by the EU as conflicting with a 'European' identity based on values of peace and democracy. While it appears all but inconceivable that Turkey could become an EU member with the Cyprus conflict unresolved, the opposite is also true. A solution without accession also appears all but impossible. Firstly, no Turkish government could survive major concessions on this sensitive national cause without winning equally major gains in return. Secondly, as our study makes clear, substantive change in Turkey's Cyprus policy is dependent on democratisation. However, as the current crisis graphically underlines, the latter evokes powerful resistance which may not easily be overcome in a purely domestic contest. As the post-Helsinki experience shows, the only European incentive strong enough to anchor domestic democratisation is a clear and credible commitment to EU entry. But for the past few years, the alliance between the EU and domestic reformers, which for a brief period achieved significant change, has been undergoing a crisis of confidence on both sides. Its re-establishment on a firmer basis appears to be a prerequisite for a Cyprus solution—and for Turkey's European future.

INDEX